Spiritual abuse is one of the greatest stains on the bride of Christ today. Too few with pulpits and platforms are willing to recognize the basic truths that Michael Kruger addresses clearly, convincingly, and biblically. I thought *Bully Pulpit* would be a book every pastor and Christian leader ought to read. But I changed my mind: every Christian from pulpit to pew needs to read this wise and timely work—for the sake of the church and her people.

KAREN SWALLOW PRIOR, research professor of English
and Christianity & Culture at Southeastern Baptist
Theological Seminary and author of *On Reading Well*

Who would ever have thought we would reach a point in the life of the church where the adjective *bully* would modify the noun *pulpit?* Yet, sadly, we have arrived. This book is both urgent and timely, as the presence of domineering and abusive church leaders continues to make headlines. This book is not only for pastors and elders but should be read by all Christians who care about the life and health of the body of Christ. I highly recommend it.

SAM STORMS, lead pastor for preaching and vision at Bridgeway
Church and author of *Understanding Spiritual Gifts*

With prophetic courage and pastoral compassion, Mike Kruger has written an important book on a difficult subject. No one likes to think or talk about spiritual abuse, especially in the church, but if we neglect and ignore this very real problem and don't find the right ways to confront it, woe to us. So if you're a church leader who wants to shepherd the precious flock of God in the paradigm, pattern, and posture of the Chief Shepherd, Jesus Christ, pick up this must-read book, then listen and learn.

JULIUS J. KIM, PhD, president of the Gospel Coalition

The apostle Paul tells us the overseer of God's people is not to be a bully, but gentle (1 Tim. 3:3, CSB), and yet we too often overlook significant character issues or actions that should be disqualifying for ministry because of how God seems to be using an individual or growing a church. *Bully Pulpit* provides wise and measured reflections on the reality of shepherds who reject Christ's vision of leadership and leave spiritual destruction in the wake of their sin. I hope this important book prompts serious discussion among God's people.

> TREVIN WAX, vice president of research and resource development
> at the North American Mission Board and visiting professor
> at Cedarville University, author of *The Thrill of Orthodoxy*

Learned and wise, urgent and timely, biblical and hopeful—this book deals with a sensitive topic with enormous skill and care. I can think of no better book on the subject and hope it will be read widely.

> SAM ALLBERRY, pastor and author of *Why Bother with Church?*

This book is not a reaction but a response. Reactions to spiritual abuse are understandably passionate, but often without constructive insight. Dr. Kruger responds with both passion and constructive insight into both how leadership dynamics often deny the character of our Lord Jesus and how building new dynamics will put that very character on vibrant display.

> JEREMY PIERRE, Lawrence & Charlotte Hoover Professor
> of Biblical Counseling Chair, Department of Biblical
> Counseling and Family Ministry at The Southern Baptist
> Theological Seminary and author of *When Home Hurts*

The topic of spiritual abuse needs careful attention and sober reflection, so I'm thankful for this thoughtful, wise, and biblical book. Dr. Kruger provides helpful clarity on a controversial subject while courageously cautioning ministry leaders about the kind of leadership that doesn't reflect the heart of Christ. Anyone who serves the spiritual needs of people should read this timely book.

> MARK VROEGOP, lead pastor of College Park Church
> and author of *Dark Clouds, Deep Mercy*

I have been waiting for a book like this that I can assign for my seminary courses on abuse. Michael has brought much needed clarity and wisdom to the devastating reality of spiritual abuse. Michael's perspective as a Bible scholar and seminary president is invaluable. He brings church leaders face-to-face with the destruction abusers cause. He does this to help us take spiritual abuse seriously, to foster the motivation to enact real change, and to fill us with compassion for those who suffer from abusive "leaders."

JUSTIN S. HOLCOMB, Episcopal priest, seminary professor, and coauthor of *God Made All of Me*

While exposing spiritual abuse has become commonplace in American Christianity, few offer constructive solutions or practical wisdom. In this book Michael Kruger diagnoses the problem of spiritual abuse, describes what it is (and is not), and equips leaders to prevent abuse as well as respond appropriately when it happens. I hope every pastor reads this book and that it leads to faithfully representing our Lord, who used his power to serve.

JEREMY TREAT, pastor for preaching and vision at Reality LA and author of *Seek First*

Michael has written a courageous book for such a time as this. I pray he is a prophet who is accepted and welcomed in his own country, particularly within a Reformed and Presbyterian community not immune to this pervasive plague within the church.

REV. CHUCK DEGROAT, PhD, professor of pastoral care and Christian spirituality at Western Theological Seminary

BULLY PULPIT

BULLY PULPIT

Confronting the Problem of
Spiritual Abuse in the Church

MICHAEL J. KRUGER

ZONDERVAN
REFLECTIVE

ZONDERVAN REFLECTIVE

Bully Pulpit
Copyright © 2022 by Michael J. Kruger

Requests for information should be addressed to:
Zondervan, *3900 Sparks Dr. SE, Grand Rapids, Michigan 49546*

Zondervan titles may be purchased in bulk for educational, business, fundraising, or sales promotional use. For information, please email SpecialMarkets@Zondervan.com.

ISBN 978-0-310-13640-8 (audio)

Library of Congress Cataloging-in-Publication Data

Names: Kruger, Michael J., author.
Title: Bully pulpit : confronting the problem of spiritual abuse in the church / Michael J. Kruger.
Description: Grand Rapids : Zondervan, 2022.
Identifiers: LCCN 2022021311 (print) | LCCN 2022021312 (ebook) | ISBN 9780310136385 (hardcover) | ISBN 9780310136392 (ebook)
Subjects: LCSH: Christian leadership. | Christianity—Psychology. | Psychological abuse—Religious aspects—Christianity. | BISAC: RELIGION / Christian Living / Leadership & Mentoring | RELIGION / Christian Living / Social Issues
Classification: LCC BV652.1 .K78 2022 (print) | LCC BV652.1 (ebook) | DDC 261.8/327—dc23/eng/20220705
LC record available at https://lccn.loc.gov/2022021311
LC ebook record available at https://lccn.loc.gov/2022021312

Cover design: Derek Thornton / Notch Design
Cover photo: © Michael Marquand / Alamy Stock Photo
Interior design: Sara Colley

Printed in the United States of America

22 23 24 25 26 27 28 29 30 31 32 /TRM/ 15 14 13 12 11 10 9 8 7 6 5 4 3 2 1

CONTENTS

ACKNOWLEDGMENTS

Needless to say, this volume involved more people than just myself. So thanks are in order. First, let me express gratitude to Kyle Rohane, Jesse Hillman, Kim Tanner, and the whole team at Zondervan. They showed a keen interest in this volume from the start, and it has been a joy to work with them. A number of folks read portions of this book and provided invaluable feedback, for which I am grateful. My teaching assistant, Josh Duemler, deserves a special word of thanks for his diligent research and ability to track down sources. As with any of the books I have written, my wife Melissa has been a tremendous support. While her sharp literary eye and theological wisdom have been an incalculable blessing, her regular prayer and encouragement has kept me going during such a weighty project. It couldn't have happened without her. Most of all, I want to express my deep gratitude for all the victims of spiritual abuse who shared their stories with me. Their bravery has been an inspiration. I dedicate this book to them in hopes that there will be fewer such cases in the future because they were willing to speak up.

INTRODUCTION

I never expected to write a book on Christian leadership. And I certainly never expected to write this one. After all, my prior writing projects have been more on the academic side of the spectrum—mainly on early Christianity and the origins of the New Testament—and not on practical aspects of Christian ministry. Moreover, there hardly seems to be a gap in the market when it comes to books on Christian leadership. One might even say Christians like to write (and talk) about leadership an awful lot. I saw little need to add another voice to the mix.

In addition, were I to write a book about leadership, I would not have expected it to be about *bad* leaders. People—myself included—prefer to read books about good leaders; they would rather think positively about what leaders can and ought to be. No one likes a harbinger of bad news. Even Gandalf was criticized for being a "Stormcrow."

But sometimes God leads you down pathways you never imagined you would take. And sometimes you do things not because you want to but because they need to be done. That is the case with this book. I suppose God could have led many other people besides me to write it. But a number of factors have placed this problem of spiritual abuse squarely in my path. It's a roadblock I would have preferred to circumnavigate (and believe me, I tried). But now I know I am clearly being called to address this issue head-on.

Having spent nearly my entire ministerial career training future leaders of the church—more than twenty years as a seminary professor and a decade as a seminary president—I am more troubled than ever about the trajectory we are on. It's not just the high-profile national leadership failures over the last decade that worry me, as concerning as those are.[1] It's also the rising number of abusive leadership cases I've seen in my own circles, some of which have been gut-wrenchingly disturbing and profoundly sad. I have seen the ugliness of spiritual abuse in ways that I cannot ever unsee. And because I love the church—Christ's own bride—I am now compelled to do something about it.

Let me state the problem simply. Some of the leaders we are producing—and, if we are honest, some of the leaders we are *wanting*—have characteristics that are either absent from or completely opposed to the list of leadership characteristics laid out in Scripture. We have tolerated and even celebrated precisely the kinds of leaders Jesus warned us against: "Rulers of the Gentiles *lord it over* them. . . . But it shall not be so among you" (Mark 10:42–43, emphasis mine). Such leaders embody the essence of spiritual abuse—they are domineering, authoritarian, and heavy-handed in the way they rule those under their care.

Indeed, Jesus spent a remarkable amount of time warning God's people against bad leaders—something the modern church would do well to remember.

The church can be like the nation of Israel in that we sometimes don't want a king with the qualities God desires but prefer a king like "all the other nations have" (1 Sam. 8:5 NIV). We want leaders who are powerful, decisive, inspiring, dynamic, and get things done. Even though God warns us that such leaders might rule us harshly—he warned Israel that they would be the king's "slaves"

(1 Sam. 8:17)—we insist that we know better. We would rather have a leader who will beat up our enemies than one who will tenderly care for the sheep.

It's not that different from the person who decides to buy a pit bull as a family pet. It may be cool to have a tough dog, and it may protect you from burglars. But eventually it may maul a member of your own family.

The temptation, of course, is to think this problem is always in *other* churches or denominations. We tend to think our little slice of evangelicalism has taken the right steps or has the proper theology to keep spiritual abuse from happening. *They* are the ones with bully pastors, not us.

But I have come to realize this is not the case. Even the denominational tribes that we might consider the most theologically solid and the most doctrinally faithful are not immune to this problem. Rather, it is sometimes precisely these groups that are most vulnerable because they often presume from the outset that the purity of their pastor's doctrine must somehow guarantee the purity of their pastor's character. Perhaps a little more humility about the former may have occasioned a little more self-reflection about the latter.

To be sure, others have noticed this problem of pastors being abusive bullies, and some have already written helpful books on spiritual abuse. (I will be referring to some of these throughout this book.) So why another book? My hope is that my role as a biblical scholar and seminary president might allow me to offer a unique perspective and perhaps provide a voice into this issue that will gain a hearing from some who may not otherwise listen.

After all, pastors have learned to tune out most criticisms of their profession, and rightly so. The office has lost its dignity in our modern culture, lacking the respect and appreciation it once had and deserves. Every day, pastors are bombarded with unjust critiques and bravely press ahead in the midst of them. It's part of the job.

But that doesn't mean all critiques are unjust. Sometimes it takes a voice from within the ranks to point that out. Pastors may be more apt to listen to someone who comes from their own circles, understands their struggles, and shares their own theological and practical convictions.

Thus, one distinct feature of this book is that I am writing *as a leader in the church to other leaders in the church*. Church leaders are the primary audience because they are the ones who can prevent spiritual abuse. They can stop bully pastors. Of course, we also need books written to the victims of abuse regarding how they can cope, heal, and forgive. Thankfully, a number of these already exist.[2] I am not so much writing to help those who've been abused (though I hope they can benefit from this book) but to help church leaders identify and stop spiritual abuse. If Christian leaders can be taught to watch for this issue—sadly, generally speaking, it is not currently on their radar—then real progress is possible.

It's important to note that the vast majority of Christian leaders and pastors are wonderful people. They are not abusive bullies but are sacrificial, kind, and gentle shepherds. Indeed, I spend a lot of time with pastors (and would-be pastors) in a seminary setting. I am around them every day. I love pastors. I am a pastor myself.

And sometimes churches mistreat their pastors rather than the other way around. Being a pastor is brutally hard. (I've been there.) They are often overworked, underpaid, and underappreciated. And I suppose other books could (and should) be written about how churches unjustly critique, attack, or malign their own pastors.

Yet the fact remains: some pastors are abusive.

Unfortunately, some churches are unwilling to face this reality. Despite the pileup of churches wrecked by domineering leaders—not to mention the merry-go-round of abuse scandals in just the last decade—some churches and pastors still take a posture of defensiveness. Rather than a response of humble self-reflection, they develop a spirit of self-justification designed to minimize the concern over abuse: maybe these church members are just resentful when someone confronts their sin, or maybe they have a particularly sensitive personality, or maybe they are the products of our modern "woke" victim culture, easily offended by any expressions of authority, and so on.

Here's my point: some churches seem to have a lot of angst over whether there might be a church member somewhere bucking church authority, but there seems to be notably less concern over whether church leaders ever abuse that same authority. In their view, if there's a problem with church authority, it's almost always that there's not enough of it, rather than it going too far.

To be clear, both mistakes—abdication of authority and abuse of authority—can be a problem. But some portions of the church seem much more concerned about one than the other. This proclivity is surprising for many reasons, not the least of which is that Jesus himself spent an inordinate amount of time confronting misuses of religious authority. (Just read Matthew 23 again.) He did not see the danger on only one side of the equation.

In some ways, the problem of abusive church leaders is not all that different from the problem of abusive police officers. While most officers are honorable, kind, and brave, some do use excessive force. And the reality of the former can't be an excuse to ignore the latter. But, sadly, to protect the "dignity of the office," abuse is sometimes minimized or overlooked—sometimes even by other police officers. Ironically, it is this misguided desire to protect the office that may actually be harming it. The dignity of the office would be better protected if more good police officers had the courage to stand up to the abusive ones.

Back in 2020 our country learned this lesson the hard way. Spread across the nation and the world was the tragic image of a police officer, Derek Chauvin, with his knee on the neck of George Floyd as he begged for help, saying he couldn't breathe. Despite the shouts and pleas of the crowd, the officer left his knee where it was. George Floyd became unresponsive and eventually died.

That image, as awful as it was, demonstrated to the satisfaction of the jury and to the majority of the public that police officers sometimes abuse their authority. Sometimes they use excessive force. Acknowledging that reality does not make a person a cop hater. No, you can believe that most police officers are honorable, kind, and brave and at the same time believe that a small minority are not. The two positions are not mutually exclusive.

But additional factors made the George Floyd tragedy particularly disturbing. For one, Chauvin apparently had a track record of abusive behavior toward those in his custody—twenty-two formal complaints over nineteen years on the force—and only one instance where he was disciplined.[3] Another factor was the other police officers standing right there who did nothing to stop Chauvin, even with George Floyd pleading for his life. On the contrary, they protected Chauvin from the crowd and enabled him to continue his abusive behavior.

Instead of protecting George Floyd, these officers protected their fellow officer.

Sadly, the same patterns of abuse in the George Floyd case are sometimes found in the church. While most pastors are gentle, kind, and patient, others have a proverbial knee on the neck of their sheep. They've been doing it for years with little or no consequences. And despite the pleas of the people, other pastors and elders sometimes stand by and let it happen. They may even defend the bully pastor. In sum, the problem is not just the abuse. It's also the larger context that allows it to continue unchallenged.

So something needs to change. For the sake of the peace and purity of the church, and for the sake of the sheep we are called to protect, we must think more carefully about the type of leaders we are producing.

This present volume is a small step in that direction. I am not under the impression (nor should the reader be) that this book can fully address the problem of spiritual abuse. There is much more to say than I have said here. But I do hope it can be a useful tool in the hands of pastors, elders, ministry leaders, and even laypeople in the church.

As we begin, a few clarifications and qualifications are in order.

- Because I am writing primarily to address spiritual abuse in the church, I will regularly refer to abusive "pastors" and to the "elders" or broader ecclesiastical bodies that surround those pastors. This is not to suggest that spiritual abuse takes place only in a formal church. Christian organizations are vulnerable to these same problems (as seen in the case of Ravi Zacharias). Thus, the reader could easily substitute "leader" for "pastor" or "board of trustees" for "elders" and find that many of the same principles apply.

- Speaking of elder boards and ecclesiastical bodies, I also recognize that there are various forms of church government, ranging from congregational to Presbyterian to episcopal. Unfortunately, I can't address all the unique features of these systems. Thus, for the sake of simplicity, I am using the broad terminology "board of elders" to signify whatever ecclesiastical body might have responsibility to oversee the church's leader. I also realize the church's leader is called different titles in different contexts: minister, pastor, priest, rector, bishop, and more. I have chosen to use the generic term *pastor*, but I am aware of these differences.

- Throughout this volume, I usually refer to an abusive leader as "he." This is done for the sake of grammatical simplicity and is not to suggest that women cannot also be spiritually abusive. I recognize that there are women in leadership roles in some churches and Christian organizations and that they too sometimes fall into these same patterns of behavior. But because the overwhelming majority of abusive leaders in Christian spaces are male, I have kept the masculine pronoun.

- Since this volume is concerned with those who have been spiritually abused, I often refer to these folks as "victims." No doubt this term will occasion some negative reactions among some, and I want to address two of them here. First, some will take the use of this term as evidence that this volume is advocating a "victim mentality" among those who have suffered injustice, a mentality which presumably means that a person is free to build their whole identity around the bad things that have happened to them, blaming those injustices for all the problems in their life. But I wholeheartedly reject such a notion. Christians are called to build their identity around Christ, not the injustices they have experienced. At the same time, there is nothing inappropriate or unbiblical about using the term *victim* to describe someone who has endured serious mistreatment. The Bible recognizes that such injustices can happen to people and that God cares about such injustices (Eccl. 4:1; Ps. 9:9). One can be a victim without being *only* a victim.

- Second, some will take the use of the term *victim* as inherently prejudicial against the accused pastor. To use the term, it is argued, assumes the victim really is a victim, and we simply don't know that. But such an objection misses the entire point of the book. I am not writing a book about judicial process— that is, the detailed steps of how to conduct an ecclesiastical trial or investigation. I am writing a book about how some pastors abuse their sheep. And whenever you talk about pastors abusing their sheep, it is entirely appropriate to use the term *victims* to describe those sheep. In particular cases, pastors should be considered innocent until proven guilty. But this book isn't about proving a particular case. It is about documenting a trend in the church and calling the church to take steps to stop that trend.

With these qualifications in mind, we are now ready to take a deeper plunge into the problem of spiritual abuse. The following chapters will seek to accomplish the goal I laid out above—namely, to help churches or Christian ministries identify and stop spiritually abusive leaders in their midst. Thus, we will explore a wide range of diagnostic topics: How do we explain the apparent rise of the bully pastor? (chapter 1), What exactly is spiritual abuse? (chapter 2), What does the Bible say about abusive leadership? (chapter 3), What causes churches to turn a blind eye to abusive leadership? (chapter 4), and What are the retaliatory tactics abusive leaders use to keep their positions? (chapter 5).

But this book is more than diagnostic. My goal is also to help leaders understand the serious damage that spiritual abuse causes in the lives of those who've suffered under it. To take spiritual abuse seriously, we must come face-to-face with the destroyed lives left in the wake of abusive leaders (chapter 6). My prayer is that leaders will let those stories sink in so that they are filled with compassion and motivated to enact real change.

That motivation for change is then funneled into the seventh and final chapter. There I lay out some practical, structural steps for how churches can both prevent spiritual abuse and properly respond to it when it occurs.

So let us begin. As we do, we can be encouraged that God cares for the mistreated even more than we do:

The LORD sits enthroned forever;
he has established his throne for justice. . . .
The LORD is a stronghold for the oppressed,
a stronghold in times of trouble.
And those who know your name put their trust
in you,
for you, O LORD, have not forsaken those who
seek you. (Psalm 9:7–10)

ONE

THE FIRST SHALL BE FIRST

The Problem of the Bully Pastor

Of all bad men religious bad men are the worst.
—C. S. LEWIS

Scut Farkus.

When it comes to movie bullies, he is one of the most infamous. In the classic film *A Christmas Story*, the red-headed Scut—wearing a coonskin cap and flanked by his shorter partner in crime, Grover Dill—torments young Ralphie and his brother on the way home from school. Audiences can't decide whether to laugh or wince as Scut twists the kids' arms until they cry, "Uncle!" (and then doesn't stop even when they do).

This comical scene has proven to be one of the most iconic of the film. In a movie with no shortage of nostalgia—it's set in the 1940s, after all—it is curious that one of the most memorable moments is watching one kid beat up another kid. And the reason is not hard to imagine. Most everyone grew up knowing a bully in their neighborhood, someone who would intimidate, threaten, and domineer the other kids. To watch that scene is to be transported back to one's childhood.

Indeed, bullies are part of the human experience. One can easily make a list of infamous movie bullies: Biff Tannen (*Back to the Future*), Johnny Lawrence (*The Karate Kid*), Ace Merrill (*Stand by Me*), and Draco Malfoy (*Harry Potter*).

Of course, bullies don't disappear when you graduate from high school. They are still around, though maybe in more subtle forms. And, perhaps most sadly, bullies are even in the church—the very spot where people should be safest.

But there's one big difference. Bullies in the church often don't look like bullies. They are not the cartoonish villains of the movies—easy to spot, dressed in black, twisting their moustache as they fiendishly plot the hero's demise. Instead, bullies in the church often look (at least at first) like the hero. They look like the good guy until we discover they're the bad guy.

Just imagine it for a moment. What if at the end of *Harry Potter* you discovered that the abusive individual was not Draco Malfoy but Albus Dumbledore? What if the abusive leader wasn't Biff Tannen but Doc Brown? That's what makes spiritual abuse disturbing and so hard to spot. It happens at the hands of those who are charged with the care and protection of the flock.

THE PROBLEM OF THE BULLY PASTOR

In 2019 Sam Allberry lamented, "A sad trend has developed in recent years: Pastors having to leave for bullying."[1] Soon thereafter, the Gospel Coalition editor Collin Hansen echoed Allberry's concerns: "This [problem of bully pastors] is the next pressing issue our churches must face. For far too long we've tolerated this kind of leadership that should plainly disqualify pastors by several standards in Titus 1:7–8."[2]

Even a limited awareness of evangelicalism over the last decade suggests these concerns of Allberry and Hansen aren't unfounded. In 2014 Mark Driscoll, pastor of the Seattle-based Mars Hill Church, resigned after twenty-one other pastors accused him of "abusive and intimidating conduct," which included harsh language, belittling staff, and "verbally assaulting" anyone who disagreed with him.[3] The *Seattle Times* reported that Driscoll had engaged in "bullying and abusive" behavior and led his staff in a "domineering manner."[4] Pastor Jim Henderson, a critic of Driscoll, described the sad impact of his ministry: "Driscoll is popularizing and legitimating spiritual bullying for young men, and is infecting thousands of young men."[5]

In 2018 *World* magazine reported on the resignation of numerous elders from James MacDonald's church, Harvest Bible Chapel.[6] The letter from the resigning elders accused MacDonald of "domineering and bullying . . . abusive speech . . . outbursts of anger."[7] In addition, the elders claimed the church had a "culture of fear and intimidation" and "left a trail of broken relationships."[8] But the remaining elders went on the attack, defending MacDonald against the accusations. They argued that the departing elders were the real problem and accused them of sinful and divisive behavior.[9]

Consequently, many members left Harvest Bible Chapel for nearby churches. Dave Jones, a pastor of one of those churches, said that over one hundred "Harvest refugees" had come to his church with signs that they had suffered "spiritual abuse" and were fearful that they might "be harmed in some way."[10]

As time passed, more and more evidence came to light regarding

MacDonald's behavior. According to *Christianity Today*, the elder board investigated further and concluded that MacDonald was disqualified from ministry because of, among other things, "insulting, belittling, and verbally bullying others" and "improperly exercising positional and spiritual authority."[11]

More recently, the downfall of Liberty president Jerry Falwell Jr. made national headlines. While Falwell's demise was most prominently linked to his sexual scandals, his tenure as president was riddled with concerns about bullying, abusive behavior, and intimidation.[12] For years Falwell's employees had endured this behavior in relative silence, genuinely afraid of him and any retaliation they might receive if they spoke up.

When the sexual scandal finally ended his presidency, many expressed concerns over why the Liberty board waited so long.[13] Wasn't the abusive bullying enough? Why didn't they stop him sooner? As we shall see later in this book, that question comes up in nearly all cases of spiritual abuse.

The story of Judy Dabler reminds us that abuse can be perpetrated by women as well as men. Ironically, Dabler was the founder of two ministries—Live at Peace Ministries and Creative Conciliation—that were designed to resolve conflict in Christian organizations. However, a third-party investigation revealed that she often protected the big leaders and powerful organizations that were paying the bills, and the victims were often pressured to reach inequitable settlements.[14] And if that were not enough, Dabler was also found guilty of abuse herself as she bullied and belittled staff and even sexually abused two seminary students.

And spiritual abuse is not just an American problem. Heather Tomlinson, writing for *Premier Christianity* magazine in the UK, tells of an organization that was set up to help victims of spiritual abuse. After opening, "they were inundated with Christians contacting them. So many people were seeking help that they had to shut down the support group, because they did not have enough resources to respond to all the queries."[15]

One of the few statistical studies of spiritual abuse also came out of the UK. Led by Lisa Oakley from Bournemouth University, the 2018 study reported that 63 percent of survey respondents said they had experienced some form of spiritual abuse, including coercion, control, manipulation, and the defense of such behavior with a "divine rationale."[16] Of course, the 63 percent pertains only to respondents and therefore does not reflect a number applicable to any particular congregation.[17] But even a fraction of this percentage would be concerning for the health of the church.

Whatever the hard numbers are for spiritual abuse, there is good reason to think most instances still go unreported. After all, spiritual abuse does not involve demonstrable physical acts like other forms of abuse, making it difficult to define (more on this in chapter 2). Even the victims know it is tough to prove. That fact, along with the inevitable retaliation they might expect from the bully pastor, makes most people prefer silence over speaking up.

Even for those who do report spiritual abuse, Christian organizations rarely prosecute it, as we shall see. Like most criticisms of the pastor, any accusations are lost in a maze of committees and processes, rarely making it to the light of day. And for the few cases church leadership does finally acknowledge, most go unnoticed by the media unless the pastor is famous or well-known.

In my research for this book, I learned just how deep the rabbit hole goes. In addition to drawing upon the countless abuse cases already documented in prior books on spiritual abuse,[18] I also had conversations with pastors, leaders, and parishioners across the country about cases they've witnessed and experienced—spanning different denominations, theological perspectives, and geographical locales—including numerous written and verbal testimonies from abuse victims themselves. I will refer to these cases occasionally throughout this book, leaving out details for confidentiality reasons. These testimonies made me realize I have seen only the tip of the proverbial iceberg. I honestly don't want to ponder how far below the surface it might go.

If we want to get to the bottom of the spiritual abuse problem, we need to spot the patterns that are revealed in these cases. To do that, we turn our attention now to one particular case that highlights those patterns in detail.

A PARADIGMATIC CASE

By all the standard metrics, Acts 29 CEO Steve Timmis had what seemed to be a solid ministerial career. Known for his strong Bible teaching, a deep passion for church planting, and for pastoring a fruitful church in England known as the Crowded House, Timmis was a natural candidate to lead a mission-focused ministry like Acts 29. He had published numerous books about church leadership, church planting, and discipleship, and many regarded him as an "effective and respected leader."[19] Moreover, he was a mentor to many young church planters who were eager to be guided by someone more seasoned than they were.

But all was not as it seemed.

In 2020 *Christianity Today* broke the story of how Timmis was removed from Acts 29 because of reports of abusive leadership, bullying, intimidation, heavy shepherding, and even threats of church discipline for those who resisted him.[20] Those who worked with Timmis stated that when confronted with these behaviors, he not only refused to receive critical feedback but would often reverse the accusations, making the challengers out to be the real problem. They were just troublemakers, stirring up dissension in the church.

Andy Stowell, a former elder at the Crowded House, summed it up this way: "People were and are afraid of Steve Timmis."[21]

During Timmis's time as pastor of the Crowded House, his heavy-handed leadership led to numerous relational conflicts resulting in members leaving for other churches. This community of "refugees" felt shamed and ostracized from their former community, often sharing their stories with one another in an attempt to find perspective and peace. One former member described the trauma of it all: "We at one point thought it was easier to leave the country than the church."[22]

Despite this growing list of problems, accountability was not forthcoming. After all, when Timmis was still at the Crowded House, the elder board (other than himself) consisted of just two younger men and his own son-in-law. Moreover, Timmis had his loyal defenders. Some rallied to his cause with the explanation that strong leaders sometimes ruffle people's feathers. It's just what happens when pastors are faithfully doing their job. People need to "give him grace."[23]

Even when five Dallas-based employees of Acts 29 brought complaints about Timmis directly to the organization's leadership, accountability remained elusive. On the contrary, according to *Christianity Today*, the five employees were subsequently fired and asked to sign nondisclosure agreements. The reason for the decision was that some "saw it as a clash in leadership styles, not as indicators of abuse."[24]

Most abuse cases would've ended right there—with the abusive leader emerging unscathed and the victims traumatized and isolated as if they were the problem. Thankfully, this case ended differently. Upon a closer examination of Timmis's behavior, Acts 29 recognized the problem was more than a style issue; it was genuine abuse. Consequently, Timmis was dismissed.

This story captures key themes about spiritual abuse that we will revisit throughout this book:

- Abusers typically have what appears to be a fruitful, gospel-centered ministry with a track record of success.
- Abuse often happens for years, leaving a long "debris field"[25] of broken relationships before it finally catches up with the abuser.
- Abuse involves domineering, bullying behavior, leaving the abused in genuine fear, especially if the abuse involves threats of church discipline.
- Reports of abuse rarely lead to accountability, as friends defend the abuser and the board (often made up of people much younger in age or experience) provides alternative explanations.
- The victims of the abuse are typically forced out and charged as troublemakers who are attacking a faithful pastor just doing his job.

The previous scenarios paint a sobering picture of how leadership sometimes goes terribly wrong in the church. If the problem of abusive leaders is even a fraction as bad as we might fear, then we cannot avoid a foundational question: How did we get here?

HOW DID WE GET HERE?

The problem of bully leaders is nothing new. Since the fall in the garden of Eden, humans have lorded over other humans in cruel and demeaning ways. Indeed, even the most limited awareness of church history reveals that the church has seen this sort of problem before (and much worse).[26] We must acknowledge that maybe there is not a rise in bullying, just a rise in awareness or reporting (likely because of the proliferation of social media). It is difficult to know one way or the other.

Even so, we can ask whether there are factors that account for the apparent rise of bully pastors in our modern day. Even if it's only our awareness that is new and even though our current generation's problems aren't unique, these are not reasons to turn a blind eye to the problem. It is still worthwhile to explore what may have gotten us here as a church. Let me offer a few possibilities.

THE CELEBRITY PASTOR

America—and the Western world in general—loves celebrities. That much is not in doubt. Whether they be athletes, actors, or successful CEOs, we are fascinated with people who are rich, powerful, and at the top of their game. And we've been taught that the way to make an organization successful is by finding an exceptional person to lead it—a franchise player—who can put it on the map.[27] Whether it's LeBron James or Jeff Bezos, all organizations need a superstar.

Given the church's propensity to mimic the culture, it's no surprise that the previous generation has seen increasing numbers of so-called celebrity pastors. Some churches want their own franchise player—someone who is strong, dynamic, and inspiring. They want someone exceptional, a charismatic visionary who can lead the way. Consequently, such celebrity pastors are often given special privileges and entitlements, regarded as specially gifted above all others, and given a voice and authority that exceed all those around them (even if churches claim these individuals are just one voice among many).

Of course, we should remember that there have been "celebrity pastors" in every age of the church. The fourth-century church father John Chrysostom lamented the pastors in his day as having the following vices: "Love of praise, greed for preferment (which more than anything else hurls the human soul to destruction), teaching meant to please, slavish wheedling, ignoble flattery, contempt for the poor, fawning on the rich, absurd honours and harmful favours which endanger giver and receiver alike, servile fear fit only for the meanest of slaves, restraint of plain speaking, much pretended and no real humility." [28] We might think these words were written in the modern day if we didn't know better.

To be sure, the celebrity pastor doesn't have to be that exceptional to expect special treatment. It doesn't matter if his church is fifty people or five hundred. He merely has to be the big fish in his own little pond. After all, athletes don't have to be in the professional leagues to have a cocky swagger about them. Even a high school football player can develop an enormous ego from the incessant praise of the hometown crowd.

With this sort of celebrity ministry culture, it's no wonder that some churches have attracted narcissistic personalities to their pulpits. [29] The job of the pastor is no longer just about being a faithful teacher and gentle shepherd. Now he is the centerpiece of the big show. As Chuck DeGroat observed, narcissistic leaders "are obsessively preoccupied with their reputation, influence, success, rightness, progressiveness, relevance, platform, affirmation, and power." [30] These obsessions are the perfect recipe for a bully pastor who will do almost anything to retain their empire and squash anyone who threatens it.

GIFTS OVER CHARACTER

Churches don't usually end up with narcissistic celebrity pastors simply because that pastor has maneuvered his way to the top. On the contrary, some churches have invited them in and built them up. As McKnight and Barringer observed, "Of course, celebrities don't form on their own. Behind every celebrity pastor is an adoring congregation that both loves and supports the celebrity atmosphere." [31]

Churches that foster such an atmosphere need to recognize that they have missed—or perhaps even ignored—the biblical qualifications for ministers. Consider the list laid out in 1 Timothy 3:2–4, 6–7: "Therefore an overseer must be above reproach, the husband of one wife, sober-minded, self-controlled, respectable, hospitable, able to teach, not a drunkard, not violent but gentle, not quarrelsome, not a lover of money. He must manage his own household well. . . . He must not be a recent convert, or he may become puffed up with conceit. . . . He must be well thought of by outsiders."

There is much to say about each of the individual qualities on this list, but here we simply want to note Paul Tripp's simple yet critical observation: "What should strike every leader about this list of leader qualities, the thing that jumps off the page, is that above everything else you want in a leader, God values character."[32] In other words, in the long list, most everything is about a leader's character; only a single characteristic pertains to giftedness (teaching). Depending on how the traits are counted, the ratio is as drastic as twelve to one.

There's nothing on this list about being a strong leader, being able to cast a vision, or being charismatic or dynamic. I am not suggesting those aspects of leadership are irrelevant, but they certainly are not the heart of God's concern for a pastor. Nor are they ever to trump God's concern over character. As the Reformer Martin Bucer noted, "It is better to take those who may be lacking in eloquence and learning, but are genuinely concerned with the things of Christ."[33]

When this God-given ratio is reversed and churches prefer giftedness over character, churches inevitably begin to overlook a pastor's character flaws because he's so successful in other areas. Leadership performance becomes the shield that protects the pastor from criticism. As Michael Jensen observed, "We frequently promote narcissists and psychopaths. Time and time again, we forgive them their arrogance. We bracket out their abuses of their power, because we feel that we need that power to get things done."[34]

Imagine a church member of relatively low influence coming to the elder board and saying that the lead pastor is an abusive bully. That elder board is faced with a choice between possibly losing a dynamic, gifted pastor (and the ministry that goes with it) and losing a relatively inconsequential church member. It isn't difficult to see which way that decision will go. Indeed, it was effectively made long before any accusations of abuse were made—when the church decided it preferred a "gifted" pastor over a godly one.

One further observation is in order. While some churches might prefer giftedness over character, others prefer correct doctrine over character. In some conservative evangelical churches, it's not giftedness but doctrine that is king. If a pastor can articulate his theology, cite the Puritans, defend the truth against the liberals, and keep the church doctrinally "pure," then character can take a back seat.

To be sure, God cares very much about doctrine, especially for the pastors and teachers of the church (for example, Titus 1:9; 2:1). But the same danger lurks here as for those churches that make giftedness the number one factor: namely, does that church ever let a pastor's doctrinal eloquence function as a shield against character deficiencies? Are such deficiencies overlooked precisely because that pastor is seen as the upholder of the pure faith?

Sadly, this happens more than we think. Pure doctrine is sometimes seen as an indicator of pure character, despite all the biblical evidence to the contrary. Thus, some people will never entertain the possibility of spiritual abuse against such a theologically sound pastor. In their minds it just isn't possible.

A CHORUS OF YES-MEN

Once churches decide they want a dynamic, persuasive, charismatic leader—who often has narcissistic tendencies—they often don't anticipate the next problem: How do we hold that sort of leader accountable? If the previous stories are any guide, the answer is "not easily."

Most churches and Christian ministries don't have a sufficient accountability structure for the leaders they hire. It's not that they don't have *any* accountability structure; but it isn't usually sufficient. Part of the reason these structures are inadequate is that they are philosophically at odds with the church's expressed vision for pastoral leadership. After all, if the church has already indicated (at least implicitly) that the senior pastor is special—he's not like everyone else; he has a distinctive voice and authority that rise above others'—how does a church then walk that back when it comes time to hold him accountable for his behavior?

But there's a bigger issue when it comes to accountability: most elder boards or leadership boards are not composed of the type of leaders who will stand up to narcissistic bully pastors. Narcissists are remarkably good at forming alliances, building a network of supporters, and laying the groundwork for a future alienation of perceived enemies. They often groom their supporters through flattery, promises, and other forms of ingratiation.[35] Most elder boards aren't prepared for this level of coordinated manipulation. Elders are usually part-time and have limited training, while the senior pastor can devote whatever time is needed to shore up his base of support.

Also, many elder boards, particularly in church-planting contexts, are filled with young elders, many of whom are serving on their first elder board. For them, the pastor is their mentor, friend, and leader to whom they owe a great deal of allegiance. All they know about ministry they learned from him. In such cases, it is difficult—relationally and emotionally—to seriously consider that he could be spiritually abusive to the flock.

In short, most elder boards quickly succumb to the pressures of an aggressive senior pastor. They aren't necessarily complicit in his bad behavior (though, as we shall see, sometimes they are). They are simply unprepared for and unaware of what is happening.

Now, this is not to suggest that elder boards, as a rule, are easily controlled by the senior pastor. Often pastors lament how difficult and stubborn their elders can be. They may even feel that they are being bullied by their elders rather than the other way around. But things are typically different when it comes to abusive leaders. Their abusive behavior is allowed to exist unchecked precisely because they are in situations where accountability is less than adequate.

Even when the board is not filled with yes-men, pastoral bullies often find a way around the board's accountability. In the case of Mark Driscoll, the Seattle-based newspaper the *Stranger* interviewed two former elders, Paul Petry and Bent Meyer. According to these elders, Driscoll tried to change the church bylaws to "consolidate all the power" around himself.[36] When the two pastors objected, Driscoll fired them from their jobs at Mars Hill and brought them up on ecclesiastical charges for "lack of trust and respect for spiritual authority."[37] Sadly, they were convicted. In the case of Petry, "Driscoll called on Mars Hill's congregation to shun the Petry family, cutting the parents and children off from all their friends in the church community they'd spent the past several years helping to build."[38] If bully pastors, to maintain power, are willing to destroy people's lives like this, then a more robust accountability structure is needed.

Now, some church traditions will insist accountability isn't a problem for them. "*Our* form of church government protects against exactly these sorts of problems," they might say. This is often the case with denominations that emphasize a plurality of elders or higher levels of accountability (for example, bishops or church courts). But these forms of government don't magically solve the problem. Indeed, many of the abuse cases I've seen come from precisely these circles.

A MISUNDERSTANDING OF AUTHORITY

Ever since the founding of our nation, Americans haven't been particularly good at submitting to authority. The motto on the Virginia state seal—*Sic semper tyrannis* ("Thus always to tyrants!"), written beneath a picture of a Greek goddess with her foot on top of a vanquished oppressor—captures this revolutionary spirit. Fast-forward to the cultural upheaval of the 1960s, combined with an emerging postmodernity that breeds suspicion of all institutions, and one could say we live in the definitive anti-authority age.[39]

As if being a church leader weren't hard enough, this cultural context makes it particularly complicated. After all, church leaders have real, God-given authority, and church members are clearly called to submit themselves to that authority (Heb. 13:17).

But as the church has faced this anti-authority culture, two extremes have taken hold. Some churches have abandoned their leadership responsibilities, shifting to a more "organic" form of ministry where there's little accountability or oversight of the flock. Other churches have gone the opposite direction and, intent on preserving their authority, have decided it's best to clamp down even harder, showing people how seriously they take their authority and how they won't bow to the spirit of the age. Like an insecure father with a rebellious teenager, they figure they better "show them who's boss."

While neither option is biblical, the latter is the pathway to the bully pastor. And I fear that far too many churches, particularly in those circles that typically (and rightly) care more about authority, have taken it.

Curiously, Jesus anticipated this very mistake in his leaders. In Mark 10:35–45 (a passage we will revisit in chapter 3), James and John come to Jesus asking for positions of power and authority: "Grant to us to sit, one at your right hand and one at your left" (v. 37). These are the same two brothers who, after seeing a Samaritan village reject Jesus's authority, asked, "Lord, do you want us to tell fire to come down from heaven and consume them?" (Luke 9:54). James and John's leadership model is clear. If someone doesn't respect your authority, you drop the hammer. Problem solved.

But Jesus's model for ministry is different. After James and John's audacious request for authority, Jesus reminds the disciples that gentiles (read "unbelievers") think this way about authority: "Rulers of the Gentiles *lord it over* them, and their great ones exercise authority over them" (Mark 10:42, emphasis mine). In other words, Jesus knows that the default position for those in authority is to domineer and squash those they lead. Then comes the punch line: *"But it shall not be so among you.* But whoever would be great among you must be your servant, and whoever would be first among you must be slave of all" (vv. 43–44, emphasis mine).

Jesus's ministry model is paradoxical. You don't lead by demanding your rights but by giving them up. For the bully pastor, the first will be first. But for the godly pastor, the first shall be last. As Paul Tripp put it, "Jesus reminds the disciples that they haven't been called to lordship but to servanthood."[40]

But do most pastors view their calling as one of servanthood? Is that how most churches view the pastor's role? There may be too few that do. And that could explain (at least partially) the prevalence of bully pastors. Maybe we have hired men more eager to call down thunder than to don the servant's towel and wash people's feet.

A POSTURE OF DEFENSIVENESS

If the last twenty years has been marked by the problem of bully pastors, it has also been marked by an unprecedented amount of criticism directed at the church. We aren't just talking about the standard criticism from the secular world (though there is plenty of that to go around). Rather, there is more and more criticism from professing Christians who are tired of, frustrated by, and ready to give up on the local church.

The book titles say it all: *Life after Church, Quitting Church, They Like Jesus but Not the Church*, and *You Lost Me: Why Young Christians Are Leaving Church . . . And Rethinking Faith*.[41] And that's just the publishing world. A quick glance through a social media feed reveals that the church is in the crosshairs like never before. People feel quite free to vent their frustrations about the church for all the world to see.

As a result, it is understandable why some church leaders have adopted an overall posture of defensiveness. They might feel that it's time to defend their fellow pastors and elders. It's time to circle the wagons and stand up for the integrity of the office. It's time to show people that the church has good leaders doing the best job they can.

Given this situation, you can see why churches may not be able to hear the legitimate cries of spiritual abuse coming from their people. Such cries are lost in a white noise of critique and pushed aside as yet another instance of unjustified church bashing from those affected by an ungrateful, overly sensitive, and therapeutic culture.

No doubt, some will receive this book in precisely that manner. In some people's minds, it is yet another example of unduly airing the church's dirty laundry. The last thing we need, they might argue, is another anti-church book to stoke the fires of discontent. If we love the church, we should stop pointing out all its problems.

I understand these sentiments. Becoming disillusioned and jaded about the church is easier than we think. We have to be careful we don't slide, perhaps imperceptibly, from constructive critiques toward unbridled cynicism. Yet the opposite problem is a danger too. Fear over unbridled cynicism has caused some to put on the blinders, refusing to see and acknowledge the problems that are really there. We can convince ourselves that loving the church means keeping our mouths shut about its weaknesses.

But what if that's not what it means to love the church? What if loving the church means we want it to be sanctified so it reflects

Christ's beauty even more? What if loving the church means loving the sheep—whom Christ loves—and guarding them against the wolves Christ asked us to watch out for? What if loving the church means addressing the things that mar its reputation in front of a watching world?

In other words, that the church is the beloved bride of Christ is not a reason to care less about her shortcomings; it's a reason to care *more*. Indeed, the church is the most important institution on the planet. My prayer is that we can move past these defensive postures that might have built up from the unjust critiques over the last generation so we can hear the *just* critiques. We need to stop thinking like lawyers—ready to litigate and rebut each and every attack—and instead be willing to hear the truth if it is spoken in our midst.[42]

In the Old Testament, the prophets were less concerned with defending Israel from criticisms and more concerned with calling Israel to repent of its own sins. This didn't make them "church bashers" (or, in this case, "Israel bashers"). Judgment doesn't begin with the world; it begins with the house of God (1 Peter 4:17). Why? John Chrysostom said it best: "Christians damage Christ's cause more than his enemies and foes."[43]

In sum, perhaps we are blind to the problem of bully pastors because, in general, the church needs to do better at noticing the "log" in its own eye (Matt. 7:1–5).[44] I pray we have the courage to start by taking a long, hard look at ourselves.

NOW WHAT?

I've spent this chapter arguing not only that spiritual abuse is a serious problem in the church but also that several factors have led us to this point. These factors include (1) a celebrity pastor culture that attracts and rewards narcissistic personalities; (2) a model of pastoral ministry that values gifts or doctrine over character; (3) a lack of substantive, meaningful accountability from the elders or boards overseeing the pastor; (4) a profound misunderstanding of how Jesus wants leaders to wield their authority; and (5) a posture of defensiveness that would rather litigate criticisms than heed the prophetic warnings coming our way.

Now what? We know the problem is real, and we know a little about how we got here. So we turn our attention to addressing the problem. In the next chapter, we will explore more deeply what exactly we mean by the term *spiritual abuse*.

TWO

THAT WHICH SHALL NOT BE NAMED

What Is Spiritual Abuse?

Fear of a name increases fear of the thing itself.
—ALBUS DUMBLEDORE

Theologians love definitions. We love to shape them, nuance them, and debate them. After all, meaning can be bound up in what seem to be the tiniest distinctions. Some of the most important doctrinal debates in church history have centered on the use of a single word. At the Council of Nicaea in AD 325, the church debated whether Christ's nature was "the same substance" (*homoousios*) as the Father or merely "a similar substance" (*homoiousios*) as the Father. The debate centered on not only a single word but a single letter! So we ought to be concerned with each and every word we use.

Even so, if we are on a quest to find the perfect word to describe something, we may find that our journey never ends. Rarely does a word (or set of words) say everything we want it to say about something. It is always limited in some fashion.

And so we come to the term *spiritual abuse*. This term can be helpful, but it also has its limitations. Some prefer it. Others may not. We will work through the complexities in upcoming sections. But we mustn't let disagreement over terminology keep us from addressing the problem.

WHAT SPIRITUAL ABUSE IS NOT

Let's begin by distinguishing spiritual abuse from other sorts of abuse.

First, we are not talking about any sort of *physical* abuse, whether it be hitting, pushing, or punching someone. It is beyond heartbreaking to see such abuse in the church today—which is more of a problem than we're willing to admit—particularly the problem of domestic violence.[1] But that is not what is in view here.

Second, we are not talking about *sexual* abuse, whether it involves sexual contact or inappropriate conversations or solicitations. While the church has made some strides to address this issue, the recent events concerning Bill Hybels and Ravi Zacharias suggest we still have a long way to go.[2]

Third, we are not talking just about *emotional* or *psychological* abuse, though there is undoubtedly a significant degree of overlap.[3] The main difference is that spiritual abuse involves a person who has an ecclesiastical or spiritual authority over the victim, whereas emotional abuse can happen outside such a context (for example, in the workplace).

It is precisely to this difference that a report from the Evangelical Alliance in the UK has offered a caution about the term *spiritual abuse*.[4] While not denying the reality of this sort of abuse in the church, their concern is primarily *legal-political* in nature: "Its use now poses potential threats to religious liberty."[5] The report reviews a number of legal cases where the term *spiritual abuse* is being applied (wrongly) to legitimate church functions. For example, if a pastor declares certain controversial behaviors to be sinful (for example, homosexuality), then some have insisted this is a form of spiritual abuse.

Thus, according to the report, the term *spiritual abuse* should be avoided because it singles out religious contexts as the key factor in abuse, inadvertently giving ammunition to those who are eager to impugn the theology or activities of the church. Instead, we should just use terms like *emotional* or *psychological abuse* to avoid these complications.

The report raises some good points, and much wisdom can be gleaned from it. I certainly share the report's concern about the word *abuse* being used in this way. Merely pointing out sin is not an instance of abuse (more on this later in the chapter). We can also acknowledge that, in the legal-political sphere, *spiritual abuse* can be misunderstood. It is not a perfect term.

That said, I am not convinced it should be abandoned entirely. For one thing, my primary concern here is not protecting the church legally or politically (though I do think that matters) but protecting the church spiritually. And the term *spiritual abuse* rightly highlights the core reason this abuse is so devastating to Christians—namely, because it was perpetrated by the very pastor (or elder board) who was supposed to protect them.[6] It is that dynamic that then leads to disillusionment and distrust of the church, and perhaps Christianity as a whole.

In other words, it *does* matter that the abuse happened in a spiritual context. To leave that factor out is to miss the whole point. If a person is abused emotionally by their boss at work, that is materially different from being abused by their pastor. And I think it's appropriate to use terminology that captures that difference.

Of course, this doesn't mean there aren't other helpful terms that can be used alongside spiritual abuse—*heavy shepherding*, *authoritarian ministry*, and more. James Bannerman's classic, *The Church of Christ*, originally published in 1868, uses terms like *spiritual tyranny* and *spiritual oppression* to refer to a pastor's heavy-handed leadership—what we would now call spiritual abuse.[7] I will use some of these other terms from time to time, but eventually we must settle on some core terminology, limited and imperfect though it may be.

WHAT SPIRITUAL ABUSE IS

If we press ahead with the term *spiritual abuse*, then a formal definition is in order. While such abuse can happen in many contexts, including marriage, my focus here is narrowly on the ecclesiastical context.[8] After considering the many definitions that have gone before, along with my own research, let me suggest the following:

> Spiritual abuse is when a spiritual leader—such as a pastor, elder, or head of a Christian organization—wields his position of spiritual authority in such a way that he manipulates, domineers, bullies, and intimidates those under him as a means of maintaining his own power and control, even if he is convinced he is seeking biblical and kingdom-related goals.[9]

Let's explore several features of this definition.

SPIRITUAL ABUSE INVOLVES SOMEONE IN A POSITION OF SPIRITUAL AUTHORITY

The hallmark of spiritual abuse is that it involves one person with ecclesiastical or spiritual authority over another. Without that authority, you might have other forms of church conflict—where one person mistreats another person—but you don't have spiritual abuse. In other words, the abuse in view here happens *downward*.[10] Johnson and VanVonderen argue, "Spiritual abuse can occur when a leader uses his or her *spiritual position* to control or dominate another person."[11] Wehr refers to this dominating behavior as "pious coercion."[12]

Lest we think such abuse of church power is only a modern or postmodern concern, we see that Bannerman plainly acknowledged this problem even in the 19th century. He argued we should limit the "power" of church leaders because "it excludes the possibility of that power becoming an independent despotism or lordship in the hands of the rulers, and of their regarding it as if it were given for their own aggrandizement and exaltation, or to be used for the subjugation, by a spiritual tyranny, of the consciences and understandings of the other members of the church."[13]

More than a century earlier, Matthew Henry lamented that "church-power and church-censures are often abused."[14] He argued that God's Word forbids pastors who exhibit "tyranny and abuse of power . . . [Because] so hard is it for vain men, even good men, to have such authority, and not to be puffed up with it, and do more hurt than good with it, that our Lord Jesus saw fit wholly to banish it out of his church."[15]

Now, to be clear, the Bible affirms the proper role of authorities—in the church and in the world. The Bible is not anti-authority, nor does it try to extinguish all such distinctions. Rather, the reason spiritual abuse is a real possibility is because spiritual authority is a real category. Some Christians have attempted to solve the problem of spiritual abuse by eliminating all authorities in the church. If we can flatten out all distinctions, then perhaps we can eliminate abuse of authority.

But that is not the solution presented in Scripture. As we shall explore further in chapter 3, the Bible doesn't solve abusive authority by eliminating all authority. Rather, in light of the fallen nature of humanity, the Bible repeatedly warns against the *misuse* of that authority (Matt. 20:25; 1 Tim. 3:3; 1 Peter 5:3). Unfortunately, some churches miss these repeated warnings. They may be so intent on defending the legitimacy of their authority that they devote little time to exploring its possible abuses.

Also, abusers often have multiple layers of authority. For example, if a pastor abuses a member of his staff, then he is operating from *two* positions of authority: he is that person's *pastor* and *boss*. And if the staff member is female, some pastors may wrongly exploit an additional male-female dynamic as yet *another* level of perceived authority (even though women are not called to submit to men just because they're men).

In churches that embrace a patriarchal theology, the weight of this authority is felt even more acutely. Although patriarchal theology should be distinguished from biblical complementarianism, some groups claim to be complementarian but effectively operate with a patriarchal paradigm. In one case I studied of a church accused of having abusive leadership, an outside organization's investigation revealed significant patriarchal tendencies, despite the church's claim to be complementarian.

These churches often have a severe top-down male authority structure that is not to be questioned or challenged, especially by women. These church cultures create an ideal environment for spiritual abuse. In a case I studied from a church in the Southwest, the abusive pastor tried to suppress a woman's concerns to the elder board by using passages like 1 Corinthians 14:34–35, where it says women should be silent in church—an appalling and irresponsible application of that passage.

Once we come to grips with these layers of authority, we can begin to grasp why spiritual abuse is so devastating. If one member of the church makes derogatory remarks to another member, the remarks can be very painful. But they lack the *weight* of an authoritative office behind them.

In contrast, if a *pastor* makes precisely the same remarks, it can be crushing in a different way. It can make a person doubt what *God* thinks of them (after all, doesn't this leader represent God in some way?), it can make them fearful of losing their job (if they are on staff), it can make them wonder whether this leader might invoke church discipline against them (especially if there is a track record of such retaliations), and it can cause concern that this leader is speaking negatively about them to other church members (especially if the pastor regularly makes negative remarks about others).

In particular, abuse survivors routinely testify that the most devastating part of their experience is the way the abusive pastor *used Scripture against them*.[16] Passages from the Bible are used to attack, demean, and control them, and those passages bear extra weight on the lips of God's appointed leader. Many victims testify that even many years later they still can't get their pastor's voice out of their head as they read the Bible.

It is also not unusual for abusive pastors to attack their victims from the pulpit. In a testimony I received about a church in the Northeast, the abusive pastor used his sermons to target individuals in the congregation, even though the congregation as a whole was unaware. The pastor weaponized his sermons to intimidate and attack his enemies.

Eerily similar is the case of Mark Driscoll's former assistant, Karen Schaeffer. After Driscoll abruptly fired her for "heresy," merely for suggesting he needed more people around him who could genuinely challenge him, he said to her, "Trust is really hard to earn, and it's really easy to lose."[17] Then in a later sermon, Driscoll talked about how he had been "betrayed" by someone close to him and repeated the same line he had spoken to Schaeffer. Knowing she was being directly targeted from the pulpit, Schaeffer immediately left the sanctuary in tears, never to return.[18]

Note that such damage does not require that the pastor *directly* invoke divine authority to justify his actions or comments. He doesn't have to say things like, "I am speaking for God," or "God told me," to wield his authority abusively. While some theological traditions might be more prone to such language than others, we should remember that it is the *office* of the pastor (or Christian leader), and the implied authority that goes along with it, that is decisive.

In sum, a pastor's words can be either disproportionately encouraging or disproportionately damaging. Pastors effectively have a "pulpit" inside people's heads. This is precisely why character matters so much when it comes to whether a person is qualified for the ministry.

SPIRITUAL ABUSE INVOLVES SINFUL METHODS OF CONTROLLING AND DOMINEERING OTHERS

As we unpack the definition of spiritual abuse, we come to a second feature: the abusive pastor uses sinful means to control and dominate those under him. When you ask people under abusive leaders to describe what this controlling behavior is like, the same words pop up repeatedly: hypercritical, cruel, threatening, defensive, and manipulative.[19] Let's say a word about each of these.

HYPERCRITICAL. A key characteristic of an abusive leader is that they *lead through fault-finding.*[20] They are overly quick to point out deficiencies in the job performance of those under them and eagerly call attention to a person's character flaws, often without gentleness or patience. Victims often indicate that they feel "watched," as if the pastor is always looking for some mistake he can grab a hold of and exploit.[21]

The abusive pastor will often defend his behavior by saying, "I am just pointing out people's sin; that's my job." But the victims of abuse know the difference between the gentle corrections of a loving shepherd and the oppressive fault-finding of an abuser. The abusive pastor denigrates others not only to feel better about himself (thus feeding his narcissism) but also to demoralize those under him. The latter is important because demoralized employees or members are more insecure, quicker to submit to commands, and eager to make amends for their perceived shortcomings. Thus, demoralization is a form of control. And bully pastors do it for one simple reason: it works.

CRUEL. In addition to always being on the hunt for flaws in others, abusive pastors often speak cruelly to employees or members. The pastor seems to *intentionally hurt* the person. This can be done by cutting off a person in a meeting, publicly embarrassing them over some mistake, making fun of them in front of others, or speaking to them in harsh or demeaning ways.[22]

In extreme cases of cruelty, some pastors are known to scream at their staff, call people "morons" or "idiots," and even swear at them. As noted in chapter 1, Mark Driscoll was known for blasting his staff with harsh language and cussing.[23] Similar accusations were made against James MacDonald.[24] The problem with these extreme cases is that they unfortunately raise the bar for what counts as abuse. Most assume that if their pastor doesn't scream and swear at people, then he must not be abusive. But there are more subtle ways to be cruel to people. While some abusive pastors use "fire" to hurt their victims, others use "ice"—they turn cold, quietly cutting off the person from the ministry of the church and from the relationships therein.

THREATENING. One of the tactics abusive leaders employ is to control those under them through threats. Only the most extreme abuse cases involve overt, blatant threats to harm someone else. But abusers are quite adept at implied threats. In story after story of spiritual abuse, the recipients of that abuse are genuinely *scared* of the abuser. Chuck DeGroat observed, "[It] is not a mild fear of these pastors, but terror. . . . These narcissistic pastors hold power in a way that intimidates and silences."[25] People are not usually scared without a reason. They must believe the pastor could really harm them. And there are several ways he can do this.

First, in a staff situation, the pastor could fire the staff member. Indeed, we saw this play out numerous times in chapter 1, with Driscoll as a key example. In the Steve Timmis case, the five Dallas-based Acts 29 employees wrote a 2015 letter to the organization's leadership explaining how Timmis often dangled the suggestion that he may no longer be able to work with certain employees anymore.[26]

Second, the pastor could bring up a person on charges of church discipline. In both the MacDonald case and the Driscoll case, the elders charged and disciplined the whistleblowers for making accusations against the senior pastor. Abusers are notoriously litigious, willing to invoke church courts if necessary to punish anyone who tries to stand up to them. This same pattern is present in numerous other cases I've studied. In one example, a couple was excommunicated for "slander" simply because they raised concerns about the senior pastor's domineering and harsh behavior.

Third, pastors can threaten to ruin a person's reputation. Even if they do not involve formal ecclesiastical charges, such threats can effectively control people. In fact, many abusive churches encourage members to openly confess their sins, insisting that they dig down deep and reveal their darkest secrets. Tragically, once these sins are confessed, sometimes under coercion, they are later used against church members who step out of line. As Kenneth Garrett observed, "In the church that abuses, the confession of sin (whether actual or imagined) is wrung out of members as means of gaining emotional control over them."[27]

Sadly, such tactics are not that different from those employed in the most disturbing non-Christian abuse cases. Harvey Weinstein not only had alleged "dirt" on those he abused, but he hired a private investigator to collect more so he could threaten and control them.[28] The difference here is that the abusive pastor can always hide behind the excuse that he was just "confronting sin" in those under him. And tragically, many elder boards accept that excuse.

Here's the point: *It is not normal for people to have this sort of fear of their pastor.* We need to let that sink in. If many people, across many years, express significant fear of a pastor, then something is very, very wrong.

DEFENSIVE. When it comes to pastoral ministry, one thing is clear: criticism is part of the job. Rightly or wrongly, every pastor will be criticized for something. But what happens when you criticize a spiritually abusive pastor bent on preserving his own authority? In short, it's war. Abusive pastors are notoriously thin-skinned, seeing even the slightest bit of criticism as a threat to their power. Case after case of spiritual abuse has shown that criticism is often the trigger that leads a pastor to turn on a staff member or parishioner, leading to retaliation, threats, and vindictive behavior. To snuff out criticism, an abusive pastor will often silence, shame, or isolate a person, making them feel like they are insubmissive, insubordinate, and undermining the church's God-given leadership.

DeGroat shared the testimony of a female staff member who had just this experience: "I was brought into a room of male elders, and the lead pastor undressed me emotionally. He told me that I was insubordinate and that if I wanted to keep my job I'd need to take a pay cut and agree to get counseling for my anger issues. My anger issues?"[29] This story is a classic picture of the abusive pastor. He accuses the staff member of insubordination and then makes *her* out to be the real problem.

Testimonies I read from a church in the Midwest described an abusive pastor who was known for flying off the handle anytime he was criticized. If a person spoke up against him on any issue, they were immediately labeled an enemy, often followed by a verbal tirade and then weeks and even months of the silent treatment. This behavior was so traumatic for the church staff that some would even tremble from fear when the pastor walked into the room.

The rich irony here is that the pastor who is unable to take criticism is often highly critical of everyone else. That is not a good combination—and it's the classic mark of a narcissist.[30] Narcissists can't admit that others may be smarter or more talented than they are, which is why they always critique others. Nor can they admit that they might be inferior or mistaken, which is why they won't allow critiques of themselves or the ministries they lead.

Another sign of overly defensive pastors is that *they continually remind people of their authority*. In such cases, pastors will often say things like, "I'm your boss," or, "I'm over you," or, "I'm in charge." On top of these reminders, there may be regular appeals to scriptural teachings about the authority of the pastor or the elders: how they hold the "keys to the kingdom" (Matt. 16:19) and that church members are to submit to their leaders (Heb. 13:17). And on it goes. Johnson and VanVonderen refer to this behavior as "power-posturing."[31]

Now, it's certainly true that churches and their leaders have authority. The Bible is not anti-authority. But, as we saw in chapter 1, that authority looks very different from the way the world conceives of it. And a perpetual drum beat on the theme of the pastor's authority should be a warning sign. An inordinate desire to prove one's authority can be a pathway to abuse.

MANIPULATIVE. Of all the qualities of the abusive pastor, this last one may be the most critical. The only way abusive pastors can survive as long as they do is if they are able to manipulate the system in such a way that they are protected and their victims are silenced. The first kind of manipulation is *structural*. Abusers often make sure certain practices are in place to preserve their authority. An example is the notorious "personnel committee," which is typically a subset of an elder board. By making sure all conflicts are handled discretely in this committee, years of conflict can go unnoticed by the larger governing body. I will address more of these structural issues in chapter 7.

The other type of manipulation is *relational*. Abusers masterfully cultivate an immense amount of loyalty from those they serve with. This is accomplished in a number of ways, usually by flattery ("You are so gifted"), by entrusting someone with a secret ("I am telling only you"), including someone in the inner circle ("Only a select few are invited to this meeting"), or even by confessing selective sins of their own (what DeGroat calls "fauxnerability").[32] In short, the abuser grooms people in a way that is not all that different from what happens in cases of sexual abuse, manipulating them to gain their trust.

Relational manipulation has a significant payoff for the abusive leader. For one, it generates the kind of loyalty he might need at a later point if ever accusations are made against him. In addition, abusive pastors often use this sort of influence to get other leaders in the church (usually elders) to engage in bullying behavior on their behalf. In numerous cases I studied—ranging from the West coast to the Southeast—the bully pastor was known to send other elders or pastors to confront anyone he saw as a threat, to accuse them and keep them in line (usually under the auspices of "shepherding"). At this point, the abuse had become systemic, now involving more than the senior pastor alone.

SPIRITUAL ABUSERS SEEM TO BE BUILDING GOD'S KINGDOM (BUT ARE REALLY BUILDING THEIR OWN)

The third feature of spiritual abuse is that the abusive leader appears to be building God's kingdom—at least on the outside—but is actually protecting his own power and authority. Spiritual abuse usually happens because a pastor is desperately trying to control his ministry and keep it on track. He wants to control his staff, control the vision, control the direction of the church. Loyalty must be maintained at all costs. Nothing can be allowed to diminish his position or take away his power. And when people fall out of line (which tends to happen with human beings), then he cracks the whip.

Again, from Johnson and VanVonderen: "It's possible to become so determined to defend a spiritual place of authority, a doctrine or a way of doing things, that you wound and abuse anyone who questions, or disagrees, or doesn't 'behave' spiritually the way you want them to."[33]

Now, this isn't necessarily the way the abusive pastor sees it. On the contrary, he may be convinced he is building God's kingdom, not his own. In his mind, he is so significant to the work of the kingdom, so important, so valuable that he feels justified in doing nearly anything to keep that ministry on track. If people get run over, then that's because they got in the way of the great kingdom work he's doing—collateral damage, so to speak. In a sick, twisted way, he is crushing people for the glory of God.

In a sense, abusive pastors are both aware and unaware of what they are doing. Yes, they know they are hurting people (though they often don't know how badly). Yes, they are doing it on purpose. But their own narcissistic illusions about the greatness of their ministry allows them to dismiss their behavior as a normal, inevitable part of the advancement of the kingdom.[34]

They have convinced themselves that their great kingdom accomplishments outweigh any damage they might inflict on people along the way.

Consequently, when abusive pastors are finally confronted over their domineering behavior, they often vehemently deny that they have done anything wrong.[35] The accusation may even shock them.[36] Yes, perhaps deep down they know they are mistreating people to maintain their own power and control. But the success of their ministries, at least in their own narcissistic minds, is proof enough of their innocence. This belief is why true repentance is rare among spiritual abusers.

Here's the reality: pastors accused of spiritual abuse are often accomplishing something helpful for the kingdom—expanding the reach of the gospel, planting churches, helping the poor. Their ministries look blessed. This appearance of blessing not only makes the abusive pastor sure that he's done nothing wrong, but it also convinces others of his innocence. They refuse to believe any accusations. To allow such a possibility would wreck the tidy world they have built around that spiritual leader.

NOT EVERYTHING IS ABUSE

So far I've laid out three features of spiritual abuse: (1) it involves people in ecclesiastical or spiritual authority, (2) it involves sinful means of controlling and dominating others, and (3) it usually involves a leader who seems to be doing great work for God's kingdom (when he's really building his own).

But just having a definition doesn't solve all our problems. *Applying* the definition is the tricky part. Not everything is abuse, so we have to make sure we don't confuse it with other problems or practices in the church. It would be equally tragic for churches or church members to turn every conflict into a case of spiritual abuse, throwing accusations around lightly and frivolously. So here are some things that aren't necessarily abuse.

BEING UNFRIENDLY. Let's be honest, some pastors don't have the best bedside manner. They can be gruff, abrupt, distant, and seemingly uncaring. They may not remember your name or reach out to you for prayer requests. Their relational intelligence may be pretty low. But these characteristics—as frustrating and limiting as they may be—don't qualify as abusive behavior.

AN INTIMIDATING PERSONALITY. There is a difference between intentionally intimidating others through threats, attacks, and bullying and just having an intimidating personality. I've met many Christian leaders who are gifted, talented, and project a confidence that makes other people feel insecure. Most often they are not the warm and fuzzy types who pass around hugs to everyone in the room. So they are often labeled as "intimidating." But that is not the same as being abusive.

NOT GETTING ALONG. When it comes to church staffs, the mix of personalities, gifts, and approaches can create complicated work environments. It's not uncommon for certain people to rub each other the wrong way and have a habit of bickering and arguing. It can be like an old married couple who struggle to get along. Such situations don't necessarily involve abuse. Even so, if the lead pastor seems to be at the center of nearly every conflict, with a "debris field" of broken relationships in his wake, then a more thorough investigation is warranted (more on this in chapter 7).

ACCIDENTALLY HURTING SOMEONE. Unlike many other jobs, the pastoral calling is filled with an inordinate amount of relational interaction. Pastors spend much of their time dealing with people and their problems. Inevitably, those interactions provide opportunities for people to get hurt. Pastors can make insensitive or hurtful comments. They might fail to follow up or forget to do what they said. Therefore, much of pastoral ministry is filled with apologies and repentance for these relational missteps. But these mistakes aren't abuse.

The reality that some people can be overly sensitive, feeling hurt over every interaction and every exchange, can exacerbate these hurtful missteps. But being hurt is not, in itself, proof of abuse.

However, the pattern (or lack of one) is key. Isolated instances are one thing, but if a pastor characteristically harms people by his words, there may be a bigger problem requiring investigation. As we shall see, a common tactic of some abusive leaders is to claim their accusers are overly sensitive—they're just products of a therapeutic victim culture. So while we can't say something is abuse merely because someone is hurt, we also can't say something is *not* abuse merely because someone claims the victims are overly sensitive.

CONFRONTING PEOPLE'S SINS. One of the least appealing aspects of pastoral ministry is confronting someone over the sin in their life. Sometimes people take it well; sometimes they don't. Either way, it can be an exhausting and draining experience. But merely pointing out such sin is not abuse. Despite the claims of our postmodern culture, it is not harmful or abusive merely to uphold biblical standards of conduct in the lives of God's people.[37]

That said, some additional clarifications are in order:

- Pastors can be abusive in the *manner* they confront sin. Even if they are correct about the sin itself, some pastors are heavy-handed, harsh, and overly aggressive in the way they address it. Indeed, my own research has shown that much abuse takes place *precisely when a pastor is confronting sin.* Remember, this is often the case with abusive police officers. Excessive force is typically used when a person has committed a crime! However, a church member should not have to be sinless and perfect to avoid abuse.
- Some pastors take advantage of church members caught in sin precisely because they know the members' accusations will not be believed. In other words, they are more apt to mistreat a church member when that person is vulnerable. If that pastor were accused of abusive behavior, he would only have to say, "Well, you know how difficult people can be when you point out their sin," and he would automatically have the backing of the elders.

- Some pastors are simply wrong about the sin they are confronting. Far too often we assume that if a pastor confronts someone's sin, then he must be right about it. In case after case I studied, the pastor's claims about people were often flat-out wrong. Abusers sometimes use accusations as a club to beat people, regardless of whether they're true. The accusations themselves are a form of intimidation and control. Even if there is some truth to the sin, abusive pastors have a vested interest in exaggerating people's sins so that they can wield more power over them. Testimonies I received from a church in the Midwest demonstrated this pattern. The abusive pastor was known for making quick accusations, often with inflated rhetoric. But when these situations were examined more closely, it became clear that things were not nearly as dire as portrayed.

All these categories are important to understand, lest we (wrongly) label every instance of relational conflict as abuse. As Ken Blue has cautioned, we don't want to "turn our concern with spiritual abuse into the Salem witch hunt of our time."[38]

That said, elder boards with a posture of defensiveness about their pastor may too quickly take refuge in one of the previously mentioned categories without taking the claims of abuse seriously enough. Since most elder boards *want* to find an explanation other than abuse, they may too readily offer one of those previously listed. So churches must be open to the possibility of abuse, and the abuse claims must be thoroughly and independently investigated (more on this in chapter 7).

Here's what we know: spiritual abuse is not as black-and-white as other forms of abuse, which is why so few pastors are held accountable for it.[39] Whether a pastor had an affair is more concrete than whether he is a narcissistic bully. Unfortunately, some will take this feature of spiritual abuse as a reason to reject it entirely (or at least to treat it with considerable suspicion). It's all too subjective, they might say. If we acknowledge this category of abuse, it will just lead to a wave of mistaken accusations against good pastors. Before we know it, people will find abusive pastors everywhere.

But sins that are more difficult to spot are still sins. Pride may be one of the worst sins, and yet it is remarkably difficult to prove in any given individual. Yet if such difficult-to-spot sins would disqualify a person from ministry (1 Tim. 3:3; Titus 1:7; 1 Peter 5:3; 2 Tim. 2:24), then the church is obligated to assess them even if the task of doing so requires more nuance and care. Can the church ignore these requirements merely because they are more subjective than others? One might argue that the pileup of churches wrecked by domineering leaders over the last decade shows that the church needs to do better in this area. We have ignored these requirements at our peril.

CONCLUSION

While the term *spiritual abuse* gets used a lot, it often remains muddled and undefined. I have labored in this chapter to clear up some of the confusion. In addition to laying out a positive definition for spiritual abuse, I have also been careful to distinguish it from other behaviors and practices that may be problematic but don't necessarily rise to the level of abuse.

Having a clear definition of spiritual abuse not only helps us spot it, but it also helps us appreciate why it is especially destructive to those who endure it. This abusive behavior is perpetrated by God's appointed leader (a pastor), for God's appointed ends (church planting, spreading the gospel), often enabled by God's appointed institution (the church and its elders), and leveled against God's own people (church members). As such, spiritual abuse may be one of the most destructive practices around. It is effectively spiritual child abuse.

Yet we must remember that God anticipated this problem. The Scriptures show not only that abusive behavior has been present throughout the history of God's people but also that God has plainly and repeatedly warned us against it. And so it is to those Scriptures we now turn.

THREE

A HEAVY YOKE ON US

Spiritual Abuse and the Qualifications for Ministry

No one does more harm in the Church than he who has the title or rank of holiness and acts perversely.
—GREGORY THE GREAT

They say few things are more disheartening than meeting your hero. We think we know what the celebrities, sports stars, or famous actors we admire are like (or should be like). Surely they are kind, funny, and warmhearted—just like the characters they play on the big screen. But often those expectations are quickly squashed by a rude comment, a door slammed in your face, or a gruff refusal to sign an autograph. Then we realize our hopes were profoundly misplaced.

Thankfully, most of us overcome this sort of disillusionment rather quickly. After all, we often have a low emotional investment in whether our favorite athlete is a jerk. But the same isn't usually true in the church. Whether our pastors are the kind of people they ought to be matters very much to us. Sure, everyone is a sinner who falls short of the glory of God—pastors included. But most people give their pastors quite a bit of latitude to be real people, warts and all. They aren't looking for somebody perfect, just somebody *genuine*. In a world with leaders who are sometimes cruel hypocrites, they just want a reason—even a little reason—to hope for something more.

So when people realize their leaders are abusive and oppressive, it can be spiritually debilitating and disillusioning in profound and unique ways. The person supposedly representing Jesus is nearly the opposite of Jesus. And that makes people wonder whether this whole Christianity thing may also be a fraud.

As we shall see, the presence of abusive leaders does not surprise God. The history of God's people is full of them. But he is keen to warn us against them so we can take appropriate action to protect the church. Jesus himself spent a remarkable amount of time calling out bad leaders who mistreated God's sheep. So let us turn to some key biblical passages that address this theme.

SPIRITUAL ABUSE IN THE OLD TESTAMENT

As noted in chapter 2, this book is concerned with spiritual abuse in an "ecclesiastical context." Thus, we should not be surprised that most of the relevant examples come from New Testament passages. But we can observe similar kinds of abusive leadership even during the time of the Old Testament, whether at the hands of kings, priests, or other spiritual leaders. Setting this backdrop reminds us that spiritual abuse is not so much a church problem as it is a *human* problem that has affected every age.

IN THE BEGINNING

It's fitting to begin where all human problems begin—namely, at the fall in the garden of Eden. Before Adam and Even sinned, the world was not only a harmonious place physically—no death, disease, or suffering—but it was also a harmonious place relationally. We are told, "The man and his wife were both naked and were not ashamed" (Gen. 2:25).

Of course, things didn't stay that way. After their rebellion, God pronounced his judgment on all the physical world, which involved cursing the ground and multiplying pain in childbirth (Gen. 3:16–18). He also passed judgment on the relational world, most directly affecting the only people on the planet at the time: Adam and Eve. God said to the woman, "Your desire will be for your husband, and he will *rule over* you" (Gen. 3:16 NIV, emphasis mine). The relationship that was once harmonious is now broken. The phrase *rule over* almost certainly refers to the tendency of husbands to sinfully "dominate" their wives.[1] A legitimate role of leadership becomes a weapon as it's wielded in a heavy-handed, domineering manner—a trend that would not stop with Adam and Eve.

Later we read the story of Abigail, whose husband, Nabal, had these same authoritarian tendencies. He is described as "harsh and badly behaved" (1 Sam. 25:3), and she seems to live in fear of him (1 Sam. 25:36). And in New Testament times, Paul recognized that husbands would have this tendency toward dominating leadership when he said, "Husbands, love your wives, and do not be harsh with them" (Col. 3:19).

We should also remember that Adam was not merely the first husband. As Greg Beale has argued, the garden of Eden had notable parallels to the form and function of Israel's temple.[2] In a sense, then, Eden was the first "archetypal temple in which the first man worshipped God."[3] Consequently, Adam functioned not only as a husband but also as the first priest-king, God's vice-regent on earth.

So the fall had implications for more than husband-wife relationships. It also had implications for the way priest-kings would rule and govern. Going forward, husbands would need to guard against sinfully dominating their wives, and priests and kings would need to guard against harshly ruling their people. Sadly, much of the history of Israel would be characterized by priests and kings making exactly this mistake.

A KING TO RULE OVER US

As just noted, the trend toward authoritarian leadership is not limited to the behavior of husbands. It is a danger for anyone in authority. After the Israelites had finally made it to the promised land, they clamored for a king—not just any king, but one like "all the other nations have" (1 Sam. 8:5 NIV). What did that mean? It meant they wanted a king who would "go out before us and fight our battles" (1 Sam. 8:20).[4] In other words, they wanted the typical, worldly profile of a leader: one who is strong, tough, dynamic, and powerful.[5] They would rather have a leader to beat up their enemies than one who would care for the sheep.

God, of course, was not pleased with this request. Not only was it a rejection of God himself (1 Sam. 8:7), but he had warned Israel that these sorts of leaders reign harshly and abusively: "These will be the ways of the king who will reign over you: he will take your sons. . . . He will take your daughters. . . . He will take the best of your fields and vineyards. . . . And you shall be his slaves" (1 Sam. 8:11, 13–17). These leaders are not the kind who give but the kind who take.[6] They do not care for the people but care only for themselves.

The lesson here is sobering. Sometimes the kind of leader God's people want may be the opposite of what they need. But these sorts of lessons can only be learned the hard way. So God granted their request.

Unfortunately, Israel would go on to suffer under many abusive kings. Most notable, perhaps, is the account of Rehoboam, the son of Solomon. The people cried out to him for relief: "Your father made our yoke heavy. Now therefore lighten the hard service of your father and his heavy yoke on us" (1 Kings 12:4). The older, wiser advisors told Rehoboam he should be a gentle servant leader to his people: "Serve them, and speak good words to them when you answer them, then they will be your servants forever" (1 Kings 12:7). But Rehoboam listened instead to the young men who had grown up with him and "answered the people *harshly,*" saying, "My father made your yoke heavy, but I will add to your yoke. My father disciplined you with whips, but I will discipline you with scorpions" (1 Kings 12:13–14, emphasis mine).

It's hard to imagine a clearer picture of heavy-handed, author-itarian leadership.[7] Instead of a gentle shepherd, Israel had a harsh and oppressive task master. In effect, he had his knee on Israel's neck. And Rehoboam's behavior eventually led to civil war for Israel and the dividing of the kingdom.

SHEPHERDS OF ISRAEL

God loves his children. And like any good father, he is upset when they aren't treated well. In Ezekiel 34, God lays out a par-ticularly scathing rebuke of the "shepherds of Israel"—a reference to various leaders of the people, primarily civil rulers (kings) but probably also spiritual rulers (priests and Levites). The role of a shep-herd was well-known in the ancient world—it was primarily one of protection and care for the sheep.[8] And such activity required great sacrifice from the shepherd.

Remarkably and tragically, these bad shepherds of Israel had *reversed* the roles entirely. Instead of offering protection and care for the sheep, they provided it for themselves. Instead of giving their own lives as a sacrifice, they sacrificed the lives of the sheep. One might say they were the quintessential example of spiritual abuse.

As Timothy Laniak observed, this passage is "a picture of sheep that are abused by those charged to care for them."[9]

God's rebuke of these bad shepherds has two parts: sins of *omission* (what the shepherds didn't do but should have) and sins of *commission* (what the shepherds did do but shouldn't have).[10] In terms of omission, the shepherds did not feed the sheep (v. 3), did not heal the sick and wounded sheep (v. 4), and did not seek after the lost sheep (v. 4). In terms of commission, the bad shepherds fed themselves (v. 2), clothed themselves (v. 3), and ruled the sheep "with force and harshness" (v. 4). This last phrase is typical of abusive shepherds. It's not just that they failed to care for the sheep; rather, their domineering authoritarian leadership style proactively *wounded* them. Again, as Laniak observed, "The details in this account convey how extreme the abuse had become."[11]

A few verses later, God sums up his complaint: "My sheep have become food for all the wild beasts, since . . . the shepherds have fed themselves, and have not fed my sheep" (v. 8).

Thankfully, unlike the prior passages that described abusive leadership, this passage ends on a redemptive note. God was going to *do* something about bad shepherds: "Behold, I am against the shepherds. . . . I will rescue my sheep from their mouths" (v. 10). How would he do this? By sending new shepherds? No, by coming himself to be the Great Shepherd: "I myself will be the shepherd of my sheep, and I myself will make them lie down, declares the Lord God" (v. 15).

With this promise in mind, the words of Jesus take on new significance: "I am the good shepherd. The good shepherd lays down his life for the sheep" (John 10:11). Jesus is declaring that he is the Lord God keeping the promise of Ezekiel 34 to shepherd his people. And he will do the opposite of what the bad shepherds of Israel did. They saved their lives at the expense of the sheep, whereas Jesus will save the sheep at the expense of his own life.

Other Old Testament passages also anticipate Christ's coming as the new and better shepherd. In Jeremiah 23 God warns the bad shepherds again: "Woe to the shepherds who destroy and scatter the sheep of my pasture!" (v. 1). They have mistreated the sheep in the same ways: "You have scattered my flock and have driven them away, and you have not attended [*pāqad*] to them" (v. 2). But then, in a curious play on words, God promises to attend to them in judgment: "Behold, I will attend [*pāqad*] to you for your evil deeds" (v. 2).

But God does more than judge the bad shepherds. He also promises again that he will do something to make things right. He will send a new and better shepherd: "Behold, the days are coming, declares the Lord, when I will raise up for David a righteous Branch, and he shall reign as king and deal wisely, and shall execute justice and righteousness" (v. 5). In other words, he will be a just and good shepherd for the people. Who is this righteous branch of David? This is none other than Jesus, the Messiah, the "Son of David" (Matt. 9:27).

HE DID NOT RESTRAIN THEM

When one thinks of bad shepherds in the nation of Israel, there is one story that perhaps stands out above the rest: Hophni and Phinehas. These two sons of Eli were priests in the household of God and charged with leading in worship. Instead, we are told that they were "worthless men" who "lay with the women who were serving at the entrance to the tent of meeting" (1 Sam. 2:12, 22). In other words, they were shepherds who sexually abused the sheep.

But it wasn't just sexual abuse. Hophni and Phinehas also abused their position as priests by taking the choice meats for themselves, rather than offering them to the Lord (1 Sam. 2:14–15).[12] As Ezekiel 34 described, these shepherds were busy feeding themselves rather than feeding the sheep. Most likely this was something their father Eli had already been doing for years since we are told that Eli was grossly overweight from "fattening" himself off the choicest morsels (1 Sam. 2:29; 4:18).

It gets worse. The individual bringing the sacrifice would sometimes challenge Hophni and Phineas's bad behavior. That person would recognize something was amiss and would resist giving the best meat to the priests rather than to the Lord. And what was done in response? The servant of Hophni and Phineas would threaten the person bringing the sacrifice: "No, you must give it now, and if not, I will take it by force" (1 Sam. 2:16).

We see that the problem with Hophni and Phinehas was not just sexual abuse but also what we are calling *spiritual abuse* (the two often go hand in hand). They were shepherds who bullied the sheep; they intimidated them to get what they wanted. They even had servants who helped them do their dirty work.

God was understandably enraged at these bad shepherds: "It was the will of the LORD to put them to death" (1 Sam. 2:25). What is noteworthy is that God also held Eli accountable for the bad behavior of Hophni and Phinehas. Later we are told about God's judgment on Eli: "I am about to punish his house forever, for the iniquity that he knew, because his sons were blaspheming God, and *he did not restrain them*" (1 Sam. 3:13, emphasis mine).

Here we see a critically important principle: God will hold accountable not only the bad shepherds but also those who protect and enable them. This is a weighty warning to all churches and the elder boards that lead them. Those who prop up bad leaders and turn a blind eye to their abusive behavior will someday have to give an account of their own actions.

Thankfully, as Ezekiel already indicated, the Israelites had a reason to stay hopeful. God would one day send the Good Shepherd to care for his people. But Christ knew the tendency toward abusive leadership would still be a danger, even after he had come. We now turn to a number of New Testament passages that offer even clearer warnings against authoritarian, spiritually abusive leadership.

SPIRITUAL ABUSE IN THE NEW TESTAMENT

As we turn our attention to the New Testament, we discover passages about heavy-handed leadership that are more immediately applicable to the church today. Jesus himself spends an inordinate amount of time critiquing bad leaders in first-century Israel and calling his disciples to the better way of servant leadership. Likewise, in the letters of Paul and Peter, the qualifications for ministers are addressed repeatedly, showing that Christian leaders should exhibit the qualities of gentleness, humility, and kindness.

IT SHALL NOT BE SO AMONG YOU

The first-century environment in which Jesus lived certainly had its share of harsh, abusive leaders. Jesus's own birth occurred under the reign of the tyrannical Herod the Great. As the gospel of Matthew tells us, Herod was even willing to slaughter innocent children to protect his own authority (Matt. 2:16–18). Such actions fit with what we know about Herod from other sources, which tell us that he also executed members of his own family.[13]

It's not surprising, therefore, that some first-century Jews might have had a leadership model that leaned decidedly toward the heavy-handed, authoritarian end of the spectrum. Jesus says as much in Matthew 23 when he confronts the Pharisees for their own harsh and heavy leadership: "They tie up heavy burdens, hard to bear, and lay them on people's shoulders" (v. 4). Even two of Jesus's core disciples, James and John, seemed to misunderstand the way authority works. While there's no indication they were striving to be little

Herods, so to speak, they made a rather audacious request to Jesus, as we saw in chapter 1: "Grant to us to sit, one at your right hand and one at your left" (Mark 10:37).

It doesn't take much to imagine what might have been going through their minds. If Jesus was the promised Messiah, the heir of David's throne, then that meant he would be the future Jewish king.[14] And no doubt this would be a kingdom of grandeur and greatness like no other before. James and John simply wanted to reserve their place of power in this future messianic kingdom.[15] Essentially, they called dibs on the two best seats one could have (other than Jesus's).

In response to their request for the seats of power and authority, Jesus reminded them that they were thinking of leadership in a pagan (non-Christian) way: The "rulers of the Gentiles *lord it over* them, and their great ones exercise authority over them" (Mark 10:42, emphasis mine). The key word here is *katakurieuō*—to "lord it over"—which is the same word Peter used when he rebuked harsh pastors in 1 Peter 5:3 (more on this later in this chapter).[16] Essentially, Jesus understood that those in positions of authority are prone to domineer those they lead.

Then comes the punch line: *"But it shall not be so among you.* But whoever would be great among you must be your servant, and whoever would be first among you must be slave of all" (Mark 10:43–44, emphasis mine). Jesus addressed the problem of abusive authority—but not in the way we might expect. He didn't say, "The solution here is to eliminate all positions of authority, and then there'll be no more abuse." No, Jesus called for a radical recalibration around how that authority is wielded. If a person wants to be "first" or to be "great," they don't climb the ladders of power to the best seats. Nor do they call down fire from heaven on dissenters. Instead, they must become a "servant" and a "slave"—two of the lowest positions in society.

The word translated "servant" (*diakonos*) is particularly intriguing because of the fluidity of its application. While it is often used for household servants (for example, John 2:5, 9), as well as the office of deacon (1 Tim. 3:8, 12), it is also often translated "minister" (for example, 1 Cor. 3:5; Eph. 3:7; 6:21; Col. 1:7), including Paul's description of his own labors (2 Cor. 3:6; Eph. 3:7; Col. 1:23). The nature of this word suggests that a Christian minister should be characterized by a posture of servanthood. This connection is missed by most modern churches that expect servant-like qualities in their deacons but not in their pastors or elders.

Part of the reason for this expectation is that the English word *minister* doesn't make the connection to servanthood obvious (one would have to know Greek). To capture the servant aspect more plainly, pastors would do well to use a different title (at least in their own mind). Rather than something like *senior pastor*, I suggest something like *servant minister*. These titles communicate very different aspects of the role.

If one wants to know what a servant minister looks like—as opposed to the authoritarian models the world offers—then one need only consider Jesus's final words to James and John in this episode: "Even the Son of Man came not to be served but to serve, and to give his life as a ransom for many" (Mark 10:45). In short, a life of servant ministry is not a life of gain. It is a life of death. It is not a life of power and position but one of humility and sacrifice. We want to reign on a throne, but Jesus asks us to serve on a cross. As John Calvin put it, "Christ appoints pastors of His Church, not to *rule*, but to *serve*."[17]

Maybe if we told prospective ministers *this* definition of ministry, they would think twice before signing up for such a calling. And maybe that's just the filter we need to sift out those who are not rightly suited for Christian ministry. Indeed, the people most eager to sign up for a life of power and prestige are precisely the ones in danger of becoming abusive pastors.

GENTLE AND LOWLY

The New Testament writers were acutely aware of the problem of spiritual abuse. In Paul's long list of qualifications for ministers, he is keen to mention it: "Therefore an overseer must be . . . not violent but gentle" (1 Tim. 3:3; cf. Titus 1:7). While at first glance this qualification may seem to refer to physical abuse only, the Greek word for "violent" (*plēktēs*) is all-encompassing. The Louw-Nida Greek lexicon defines it as a "person who is pugnacious and demanding; 'bully.'"[18] The HCSB captures this sense in its translation: "not a bully but gentle."[19]

The minister of Christ's church is not to be a person who accomplishes goals by manipulation or intimidation or with a demanding spirit. In other words, a spiritually abusive person is disqualified from ministry.

In addition to understanding what Paul is forbidding, we need to grasp what he positively proscribes. Rather than being a bully, a minister should be known as *gentle*. This is not a popular trait in our world today. You'll find plenty of books in the self-help section on how to be more bold, assertive, or proactive. But you will struggle to find any that are designed to teach you to be gentle. No companies looking for a new CEO have gentleness as their top trait.[20] And if a church advertises that they've hired a new senior pastor who's gentle, people aren't likely to flock to hear him.

Yet Paul believed gentleness matters very much. No doubt part of the reason for this qualification is that this trait marked the Great Shepherd, Jesus himself. Jesus described himself as "gentle and lowly" and declared, "My yoke is easy, and my burden is light" (Matt. 11:29–30). This image stands in contrast to the bad leaders of Israel who placed a "heavy yoke" on the people (1 Kings 12:4). Jesus is not harsh and abusive but patient and kind. He is not pugnacious and demanding but longsuffering and humble.

To say Jesus is gentle is to say he is "not harsh, reactionary, or easily exasperated. He is the most understanding person in the universe."[21] He doesn't put burdensome prerequisites or demands on people—heavy yokes. Or, to put it in gospel language, Jesus is full of grace (John 1:17). As for the word *lowly*, it is essentially the equivalent of *humble* (cf. James 4:6).[22] Despite Jesus's glory and grandeur, he does not separate himself from sinners with an air of haughtiness and pride. He does not have body guards and private cars but is accessible and relatable. Nothing demonstrates this humbleness better than when he literally dressed as a servant and washed his disciples' feet (John 13:4–11).

One is hard pressed to come up with two words more opposed to the characteristics of a bully pastor, which is precisely why such pastors should be disqualified from ministry. Bully pastors lack gentleness, compassion, and understanding. They put enormous burdens on the backs of people, are hypercritical, and are hardly ever pleased. Moreover, instead of being humble, abusive pastors are notoriously arrogant, convinced they (and their churches) are truly special. Not all pastors wear their pride on their sleeves. But even if it's just in their own minds, they genuinely see themselves as above others, which is why they are unwilling to receive criticism or correction.

Conveniently for us, Paul combined these two qualifications for ministry in a single verse. He wrote, "An overseer, as God's administrator, must be . . . *not arrogant . . . not a bully*" (Titus 1:7 HCSB, emphases mine). It's almost as if Paul based the qualifications for ministry on Jesus himself. If a person is not gentle and lowly, but instead a bully and arrogant, then he should not be a pastor.

Of course, to say a pastor should be gentle is not to say that's everything he should be. No one is suggesting that pastors are only gentle and nothing else. Sometimes Christian leaders should be bold and courageous, even firm and direct, especially as they contend for the truth in a hostile world (Josh. 1:18; 2 Cor. 10:5–6). The problem is that more and more churches seem to prefer only the latter. If they have a model of leadership, it's Jesus flipping over tables rather than holding the little children.

SACRIFICIAL EXAMPLES

When it comes to the qualifications for ministry, Peter has his own list to offer. He too recognizes that some leaders are drawn to an abusive leadership style: "Shepherd the flock of God . . . not for shameful gain, but eagerly; not domineering over those in your charge, but being examples to the flock" (1 Peter 5:2–3).

Just as Paul identified two negative leadership tendencies that often go hand in hand (arrogance and bullying), Peter mentions two more: *leading for one's own gain* and *leading in a domineering way*.

Peter sets the stage for the first negative trait by reminding his audience of an elder's primary duty: "Shepherd the flock of God." No doubt such language would invoke the many passages in the Old Testament where God critiqued the shepherds of Israel for their lack of care for the sheep. And what was God's consistent complaint? As noted previously, he told the bad shepherds, "[You] have been feeding yourselves! Should not shepherds feed the sheep?" (Ezek. 34:2). In other words, the hallmark of a bad shepherd is that they are in it for themselves. Peter picks up on this point and warns his audience that shepherds should not be motivated by "shameful gain."

Even the church fathers observed this problem of self-gain in ministers. John Chrysostom reminded his readers that if Paul "did more than he was commanded by God and never aimed at any advantage for himself, but only for those under his direction, was always in fear, because he kept in view the magnitude of his responsibility, what will become of us, who often aim at our own advantage?"[23]

In case after case of spiritual abuse, there is a pattern of self-protection and self-gain by the abusive pastor. It's not necessarily monetary gain, though sometimes that is the case. In addition to James MacDonald's bullying tactics, he was accused of excessive spending on himself and his family.[24] But for most bully pastors, the "gain" they seek is control and power. Sitting at the top of one's own little empire is intoxicating—so much so that they will not let anyone take it away from them without a nasty fight. This was Jesus's complaint against the abusive leadership of the Pharisees: "They love the place of honor at feasts and the best seats in the synagogues and greetings in the marketplaces" (Matt. 23:6–7).

This first negative quality—doing ministry for one's own gain—leads to the second. If someone is motivated to protect their power and authority, then that naturally leads to being willing to domineer their flocks. Peter uses the same Greek word (*katakurieuō*) that Jesus used in Mark 10:42, which literally means "to lord it over." Peter, just like Jesus and Paul, recognized that some would-be elders are quick to squash and crush those under them. In sum, Peter says that men who are self-seeking and domineering should not be elders.

But Peter is not done. Instead of just mentioning two negative characteristics that disqualify an elder, he also mentions two positive characteristics they *should* have. First, instead of shepherding for one's own gain, they should shepherd "eagerly" (*prothumōs*). This term was historically used to describe civic leaders who sacrificed their time and money for the good of the city they served.[25] So it refers to someone eager to sacrifice their lives for the good of others. Or, as the NIV puts it, "eager to serve" (1 Peter 5:2).

The second positive characteristic is also critical. Instead of domineering others, godly elders lead by "being examples to the flock" (v. 3). Leading by example is the antithesis of leading by force. Rather than intimidating, manipulating, and bullying people, the godly pastor leads by showing the way himself. In other words, he does not stand *behind* the sheep, cracking the whip, but goes *before* the sheep as an example to follow.

Of course, if a pastor is to lead by example, then his primary concern can't be controlling other people's behavior. It must be controlling his own. His own holiness is paramount. Thus, Peter is saying the same thing as Paul: character matters more than giftedness.

KIND TO EVERYONE

In all the cases of spiritual abuse I have read about, there's one word victims would never use to describe a bully pastor: *kind*. They may be many other things—dynamic, powerful, convincing, inspiring—but they are not marked by kindness. Paul, however, is convinced this trait is a requirement for those in ministry: "The Lord's servant must not be quarrelsome but *kind* to everyone" (2 Tim. 2:24, emphasis mine).

Kindness is one of the most overlooked virtues of the Christian minister. It involves a spirit of generosity and tenderheartedness toward another human being even if it is not deserved or returned. Thus, a kind heart looks to do good to another with no expectation of receiving something back. In this way, kindness reflects the very heart of the gospel. Jesus was kind to us when we didn't deserve it, so we are asked to be kind to others: "Be kind to one another, tenderhearted, forgiving one another, as God in Christ forgave you" (Eph. 4:32).

Part of what makes kindness so powerful is that we don't necessarily expect it from our leaders. We expect them to be smart and eloquent maybe, but not kind. This point was made by the 2020 breakout Apple TV+ show *Ted Lasso*. The comedy catalogs the journey of a warmhearted American football coach, Ted Lasso (played by Jason Sudeikis), who is hired to coach a soccer team in the English Premier League—despite never having played (or apparently watched) the game. Aside from the hilarious moments, and there are many, what stands out most about Ted Lasso is his remarkable *kindness* to all those around him. He is thoughtful, deferential, and focused on others. He brings gifts, remembers birthdays, and looks for little ways to care for people.

Here's the thing: his kindness *utterly shocks* everyone on the team. This is what struck me the most as I watched the show: *People don't expect kindness from their leaders.* We might expect them to be confident, focused, resilient, and decisive. And we might not even be surprised if they have a bit of an ego. But we do not expect them to be kind. How very sad.

It's worth noting that the Greek word for "kind" (*ēpios*) here in 2 Timothy can also be translated "gentle."[26] So here we have yet *another* passage—beyond 1 Timothy 3:3, and Titus 1:7—where the theme of gentleness is paramount. Why does this trait repeatedly pop up in discussions about ministry qualifications? Because gentleness is the core trait of Jesus. And it is the opposite of being an abusive bully.

Our understanding of kindness is rounded out by looking at the negative trait Paul pairs with it. We are to be kind and "not quarrelsome" (2 Tim. 2:24). In essence, this term (*machomai*) refers to verbally fighting in a way that sinfully hurts another (James 4:2). Paul is saying that an elder of Christ's church should not be verbally cruel to people—one of the defining traits of abusive pastors. This prohibition against being quarrelsome does not rule out disagreement, debate, or even vigorous theological exchanges. But it does rule out language or behavior that is belittling, harsh, or derogatory.

CONCLUSION

This chapter has offered a broad overview of the theme of spiritual abuse in the Bible. Starting in the garden of Eden, moving to the kings of Israel, and finally reviewing the role of pastors in the New Testament, we see there have always been leaders who are heavy-handed, authoritarian, and domineering. In this way, spiritual abuse is clearly a biblical category even if the precise term is not used. Moreover, like the nation of Israel, sometimes we have *asked* for leaders like this, unaware that their yoke would be heavy upon us.

When it comes to pastors in the church of Christ, however, this abusive style of leadership is a nonstarter. From Jesus to Paul to Peter, we see several important contrasts laid out regarding what a Christian leader ought to be:

- Not lording it over but being a servant (Mark 10:43–44)
- Not a bully but gentle (1 Tim. 3:3; cf. Titus 1:7)
- Not for shameful gain but serving eagerly (1 Peter 5:2)
- Not domineering but setting an example (1 Peter 5:3)
- Not quarrelsome but kind (2 Tim. 2:24)

Seeing all these traits laid out together, we are faced with an inescapable and rather sobering conclusion: many churches have been looking for the wrong kind of leaders. One might even say the forbidden traits in this list are precisely the traits some churches tolerate in their leaders. Instead, we should look for pastors who are humble, kind, gentle servants.

Perhaps there is a silver lining as we face the problem of the bully pastor. With the enormous debris field of broken relationships plainly evident across our churches, let us hope we will finally realize that a change in trajectory is desperately needed.

FOUR

A TRAIL OF DEAD BODIES

Why Churches Don't Stop
Abusive Leaders

Monsters are real. . . . They live inside
us, and sometimes they win.
—STEPHEN KING

In James Cameron's 1986 sci-fi film, *Aliens*, the main character, Ripley (played by Sigourney Weaver), discovers a little girl named Newt who is the last survivor of the human colony on the planet LV-426. Her parents and everyone she knew were wiped out by the horrifying alien creatures. After the traumatized girl finally begins to talk, she asks Ripley this perceptive and tragic question: "My mommy always said there were no monsters—no real ones—but there are . . . Why do they tell little kids that?"[1]

Children have a way of getting right to the point, asking questions that adults prefer to avoid. If there are bad guys in the world, why do we pretend there aren't? I suppose we would probably answer the same way Ripley did in the film: "Most of the time it's true." In other words, since most people are good, let's not think about the few who aren't.

Some churches have that mentality about spiritual abuse: since spiritually abusive pastors are rare, let's not talk about it and pretend they don't exist. The problem, of course, is that they do exist. As Jesus taught, sometimes the people who look like the good guys are actually the bad guys: "Beware of false prophets, who come to you in sheep's clothing but inwardly are ravenous wolves" (Matt. 7:15).

In other words, be on the watch for monsters.

Now, some may balk at the term *monster* being applied to abusive pastors. Surely they aren't that bad, it might be argued. Isn't such a term overly harsh? Well, if one prefers "ravenous wolves," then that's perfectly fine (though I am not sure there's a meaningful difference).[2] But I am using the term *monster* in a specific way—namely, to refer to the reality that abusive pastors often have two sides, like the main character in Robert Louis Stevenson's famous novel *Strange Case of Dr. Jekyll and Mr. Hyde.* One side is warm and kind (which most people experience), and the other is cruel and dark (which only the victims see). And just like in Stevenson's novel, most people can't come to grips with the fact that the same person can be both.

That brings us to the topic of this chapter. If we are to address the problem of spiritually abusive pastors—Mr. Hydes in our midst, so to speak—then we had better admit they exist and learn how to spot them. But—and here's the sad reality—it seems churches aren't typically very good at doing this. They are bad at catching monsters.

In story after story of abuse, the same tragic series of events play out. The abusive pastor engages in destructive behavior for years until someone finally has the courage to speak up. But even then, most churches do nothing. (And as we shall see in the next chapter, some churches attack the one speaking up.) Even if the church does something, it's often a half-hearted, inadequate response. When the rare church finally removes a pastor for abuse, that just leads to the next questions: Why did it take you so long to act? Why did you tolerate this behavior for twenty-five years?

The reason we ask these questions is because there is always evidence—a lot of evidence—of these pastors' destructive behavior. Chuck DeGroat, in his book *When Narcissism Comes to Church*, argues that such pastors often leave a "relational debris field" in their wake.[3] He observes, "Often, before the narcissistic pastor is exposed publicly, there are years of painful smaller encounters that are covered up."[4] These pastors have a track record of hurting those they work with, and eventually, usually after many years, it catches up with them. It is a sin pattern that can't be seen at first glance; it becomes visible only over time. As 1 Timothy 5:24 says, "The sins of some people are conspicuous, going before them to judgment, but the sins of others appear later."

In short, abusive pastors leave a "trail of dead bodies" behind them.[5] That's what monsters do. So why don't churches see the trail of dead bodies? Why don't they connect the dots? As we shall see, the problem isn't just a single, abusive pastor. Sometimes the problem is a church culture that enables (knowingly or unknowingly) the abuse.[6]

Or, as Oakley and Kinmond observed, "We [tend to] focus on the bad apple and what is wrong with it, rather than looking at the barrel in which it is kept."[7] In this chapter, we will look at the barrel.

AN INADEQUATE ACCOUNTABILITY STRUCTURE: WHAT DEAD BODIES?

The first reason some churches don't see the dead bodies is because those bodies have been hidden. The abusive pastor has buried them in the backyard, so to speak, and the inadequate accountability structure of the church means it is unable to see what is happening (and sometimes doesn't *want* to see what's happening).

The dead bodies are hidden in multiple ways. First, many victims of abusive pastors are *silenced or forced to leave.* In story after story of spiritual abuse, the recipients of that abuse are isolated and driven out of that ministry. People don't see the overall pattern because the victims of abuse don't speak out for fear of reprisal. They just leave, and the abusive pastor remains.

And if the abusive pastor remains, then he gets to control the narrative. As we shall see in the next chapter, the victims are sometimes blamed for the whole affair. *They* are the problem, not the abusive pastor.

Second, the abusive pastor's pattern of broken relationships *is often not revealed to the larger leadership body* and certainly not to the entire church. Rather, it is usually contained within certain committees or subgroups. Wade Mullen observed, "Many victims have found that their report of abuse to an organization was handled by a dedicated response team or kept within a small group of board members *instead of shared with the entire board.*"[8]

Now, some level of confidentiality is understandable and wise. Every grievance is not to be aired in front of the whole church. That said, some churches have learned to "manage" the relational debris field of the abusive pastor in a manner not that different from modern politicians—it is tucked away in personnel committees so that it never sees the light of day. So effective is this method that sometimes not even a pastor's own elders know about the long-term pattern of broken relationships, or at least don't know how deep and wide it is.

Third, even when a victim of abuse comes forward and is heard by the leadership body, the problem is often *downplayed and minimized*—it's viewed as a conflict that is inevitable in any ministry. You'll hear statements like, "Well, that's just Pastor Bob. You know the way he is." Or the problem is minimized by insisting that this is just what happens when you have a "strong leader." We see this sort of response in the case of Steve Timmis, the former CEO of Acts 29, who was eventually dismissed for spiritual abuse. His defenders said the conflicts were due merely to "a clash in leadership styles" or that "feathers get ruffled" by strong leaders.[9]

The reason minimizations like this are so effective is that they are *partly* true. Every ministry has some conflict. We live in a fallen world where clashes are part of any church.

But there is a difference with abusive pastors. The relational debris field of an abusive pastor is different not only in *volume* of conflicts but also the *depth* of those conflicts. Often the lives in his wake are genuinely destroyed; many leave the ministry and others abandon the Christian faith altogether. Also, abusive pastors often have *unresolved* conflict. They are typically estranged from many of the people they used to work with.

Once a pattern appears, the leaders of the church need to do the math. There is a common denominator in all these conflicts: the pastor. Is it more likely that *everyone else* is the problem, or that perhaps *he* is the problem?

Sadly, sometimes elders don't see the dead bodies simply because they don't want to. Despite all the holes being dug in the backyard, they just keep telling themselves that everything is all right. Why do they do this? It might be because they have a theologically incorrect view of human nature: they don't think monsters like this exist—at least not in their church.

A WRONG VIEW OF DEPRAVITY: THERE ARE NO MONSTERS

Reformed evangelicals regularly talk about the doctrine of *total depravity*—how sin is deeper and more pernicious than we realize, affecting every aspect of our lives (actions, mind, will). While every human being is not as sinful as they could possibly be, every human being—even pastors—has the potential to commit acts of serious wickedness.

Despite many churches' affirmation of this important doctrine on paper, it can quickly be forgotten when it comes to cases of spiritual abuse. As soon as victims have the courage to speak up about abusive behavior, they are usually met with a chorus of rebuttals along the lines of, "I know this pastor, and he could never do this," or, "This pastor has blessed and helped countless people over the years. He could never do something like this." Rather than taking the concerns seriously and investigating them carefully, leadership dismisses them as impossible or so unlikely as to not merit real consideration.

In other words, *monsters don't exist* (at least not in our church).

And in a tragically ironic turn, the defenders of the abusive pastor often raise questions about the integrity and the character of the victims, suggesting they are out to slander or malign the leader's "good name." So the doctrine of total depravity is forgotten when it comes to the pastor but remembered when it comes to the victims.

The revelations regarding Ravi Zacharias have shown us that even the most respected and well-loved leaders have the potential for unspeakable depravity. Zacharias's defenders argued that he could never, and would never, inflict such atrocities. But there was no shortage of evidence that he did them. Despite questionable text messages, shaky explanations, and the testimony of multiple accusers, the defenders of Zacharias stood by their man.

What explains this proclivity for churches and Christian organizations to ignore the implications of total depravity and defend their leaders, even amid concrete evidence to the contrary? In his bestselling book *Talking to Strangers*, Malcolm Gladwell provides a possible answer. Gladwell catalogs numerous high-profile criminal cases—including the sexual abuse cases of Jerry Sandusky and Larry Nassar—and shows that the perpetrators were given the benefit of the doubt time and time again, despite significant evidence of their guilt. Why? Because of what is called truth-default theory. When human beings interact with others, "we have a *default to truth*: our operating assumption is that the people we are dealing with are honest."[10]

On one level, this assumption is not a bad thing. Gladwell argues that humans default to truth because we need to do so to operate reasonably and efficiently in our society. Can you imagine if every person were routinely suspicious, doubtful, and skeptical about every other person and every truth claim? It would be a miserable, not to mention inefficient, world to live in.

But the problem is bigger. Gladwell points out that, beyond assuming that people are usually telling the truth, humans often wrongly assume they are good at spotting people who *aren't* telling the truth. We consider ourselves capable of determining whether people are lying just by evaluating their demeanor, facial expressions, and body language. But the statistics say the opposite. Gladwell provides example after example of how even law enforcement officers—police, judges, and CIA agents—are ineffective at identifying the bad guys. The combination of our assumption that most everyone is telling the truth and our overconfidence in our ability to spot liars, argues Gladwell, presents a serious problem in identifying deceptive individuals.

But the problem gets even worse. Gladwell points out a third factor in these cases: we are particularly bad at spotting bad guys when we are forced to believe something really difficult about them. He writes, "Default to truth becomes an issue when we are forced to choose between two alternatives, one of which is likely and the other of which is impossible to imagine."[11] For example, is it easier to believe that a lovable, likeable person like Jerry Sandusky sexually assaulted numerous teenage boys over the course of decades, or is it easier to believe there was just a big misunderstanding over rough-housing in the shower? The latter is much easier to accept. Is it easier to believe that a well-respected Olympic team doctor like Larry Nassar was a monstrous sexual predator, or that some of the girls misunderstood what a pelvic exam entailed? Again, many people found the latter easier to believe.

Gladwell's study can also apply to spiritual abuse in the church. Church courts—elder boards, presbytery committees—often assume they are good at spotting dishonest, deceptive pastors. But they, like all humans, default to the idea that the person in front of them is telling the truth, especially if that person has a long track record of seemingly faithful ministry. We can imagine the dilemma playing out in their minds: *Is it more likely that this respected pastor has been mistreating, bullying, and domineering his flock, or that people are oversensitive and get their feathers ruffled by a strong leader?*

The situation becomes even more complicated if those evaluating the accused pastor know him personally (which is almost always the case in church courts). If so, chances are that they have a high opinion of him. Why? *Because bullies don't bully everyone.* If they did, they wouldn't last long. Bullies rarely bully horizontally or upward. They almost always bully *down.* Thus, often the pastor has treated the people evaluating him—his peers—remarkably well.

Because the doctrine of total depravity has taken a back seat, it doesn't dawn on these folks that, as noted, spiritually abusive pastors almost always have two sides. One side is charming, gracious, and flattering. But the other side can be domineering, heavy-handed, and threatening—again, like a Dr. Jekyll and Mr. Hyde. And they are selective about who gets to see which side of them. In many ways, the abusive pastor functions like an abusive parent. Sometimes the parent is kind and loving to their child, and sometimes they are cruel and vindictive. They flip back and forth between the two personas.[12]

Can anything be done to fix this inability to see bad guys when they are right in front of us? The theological belief in total depravity should, at least in principle, help. If that doctrine were regularly taught, it should make any individual and any church court open to the possibility that professing Christians, even pastors, might commit awful acts. This doesn't mean we assume that the accused is guilty. It simply means the accusations are not ruled out as impossible. When that happens, a legitimate investigation can ensue.

But more can be done. Gladwell points out that a certain kind of rare individual is *not* hardwired to assume everyone is honest and truthful. A certain personality type goes against the grain—what Gladwell calls the "truth-teller." These individuals "are not part of existing social hierarchies."[13] Thus, they "are free to blurt out inconvenient truths or question things the rest of us take for granted."[14] In the tale *The Emperor's New Clothes* by Hans Christian Anderson, the little boy is the truth-teller. While everyone else plays along with the naked king, the boy blurts out, "Look at the king! He's not wearing anything at all!"[15]

Most elder boards, church courts, and boards of directors for Christian ministries are composed of insiders, not outsiders. They are usually composed of the leader's close friends, sometimes even family members. How, then, can they have objectivity in holding that leader accountable? It's the same problem as police officers holding other police officers accountable for excessive force. They are all part of the same club. Thus, real accountability is difficult to achieve.

What these groups need is a truth-teller, and maybe several of them. Is it possible that these Christian organizations need to recalibrate their leadership structure to include outsiders that are "not part of existing social hierarchies"? We will further explore this possible restructuring in chapter 7.

A MISUNDERSTANDING OF GRACE: EVERYONE'S A MONSTER

Christianity, at its core, has always been about grace. Paul states it well: "By grace you have been saved through faith. And this is not your own doing; it is the gift of God, not a result of works, so that no one may boast" (Eph. 2:8–9). In recent years, particularly in Reformed, evangelical circles, there has been a burst of new attention on grace. There are many calls for "grace-centered" preaching that focuses not on our good works but on the finished work of Christ. And that's a good thing.

But to accentuate the beauty of this grace, some have taken an additional step. Since we are desperate sinners saved by grace, it is reasoned, then we can make no distinctions among levels of sin. Now, more than ever, we hear phrases like "all sins are equal" or "all of us are equally sinners." Such language is intended to uphold grace; it's another way to say that no one is any better than anyone else.

Now, the phrase "all sins are equal" is partly true, depending on what one means. If one uses the phrase simply to indicate that *any* sin is enough to separate us from God and warrant his wrath, then it would be correct. God is so holy that any violation of his law, no matter how trivial in our eyes, is an offense worthy of his righteous judgment.

But that is not the only way the phrase is used. Others use it to "flatten out" all sins so they aren't distinguishable from one another. Or, to put it another way, it portrays all human beings as equally bad. If all sins are equal and all people sin, then no one is more holy than anyone else. In a world fascinated with "equality," this usage of the phrase is particularly attractive. It allows everyone to be lumped together into a single undifferentiated mass.

In other words, this understanding of grace requires us to believe *we are all monsters*.

But this belief is deeply problematic on a number of grounds. For one, to say all sins are the same is to confuse the *effect* of sin with the *heinousness* of sin. While all sins are equal in their effect (they separate us from God), they are not all equally heinous. The Bible clearly differentiates between sins. Certain sins are more severe in impact (1 Cor. 6:18), in culpability (Rom. 1:21–32), in judgment warranted (2 Peter 2:17; Mark 9:42; James 3:1), and in whether one is qualified for ministry (1 Tim. 3:1–7).

More to our point, this misunderstanding of grace has been used to defend abusive leaders. If we are all equal sinners, it is argued, then we should give these abusive pastors a break. They are sinners, just like the rest of us. To say otherwise is to put ourselves in a place of judgment over them; it is to make ourselves out to be more right-eous than other people. Instead, we need to "show them grace."

Tragically, this wrong understanding of grace is often heaped onto the backs of the victims themselves. They are chided for being "unforgiving," for "holding a grudge," or for (here we go again) "not showing grace."

It isn't hard to see how debilitating this sort of theological error can be. It makes a victim feel like they are to blame, as if their own hard heart is in the way of "reconciliation." Moreover, it utterly ignores the heinousness of the abuse itself. It forgets that some sins are worse than others. And some sinners are worse than others. And a shepherd abusing the sheep is one of the most egregious, as chapter 3 showed. Also, this misuse of grace ignores all the passages in Scripture about upholding justice and righteousness and defending the innocent.

Sadly, yet another misunderstanding of grace has been used to defend abusive pastors and further harm the victims. If we are all equally sinful, it is argued, then that must mean *the abusive pastor and the victim are equally to blame for the conflict.* A wrong understanding of grace is used to minimize the heinousness of the abuse and accentuate the sins of the victim, whatever they may be.

We all have an inherent disposition to be "fair" to both sides of a conflict. But sometimes we assume that fairness means we must find equal blame on both sides. To do otherwise would require significant time and effort to discover who's really to blame. And why bother with investigating when we already know that everyone's equally a sinner? It's much easier—and in many people's minds, even more godly—to tell both sides to confess their (equal) sins and find a way to get along.

Consequently, elder boards sometimes make statements like, "Everyone here is guilty of sin," or, "There's blame on both sides." They turn abuse into merely a relational conflict, no different than Paul and Barnabas disagreeing.

To be clear, I'm not arguing that the victims of abuse aren't sinners. They are. And I'm not saying that the victims never do anything wrong. They do. But as Jennifer Michelle Greenberg put it, "Everyone is a sinner. Not everyone is an abuser."[16]

AN IMPROPER VIEW OF RECONCILIATION: JUST MEET WITH THE MONSTER

Most elder boards or governing bodies don't like division in their ranks. Like most Christians, they want to see disputes resolved quickly—and that's good. Indeed, there seem to be more peacemaking ministries now than ever before. But this eagerness to establish peace sometimes leads churches to rush the victims of abuse into a reconciliation process with the abuser that is ill-conceived.[17] Because churches often frame the whole issue as merely a "conflict," they figure they don't need to focus on justice or accountability. Instead, they think, the problem can be solved merely by getting the abused and the abuser in a room together where everyone confesses their sins.[18]

In other words, *people just need to meet with the monster.*

But this sort of approach is deeply concerning. An abuse case is not just a conflict. It is not an equal playing field. To treat it as such is equivalent to taking a situation where a husband beats his wife and telling the couple they just need to go to marriage counseling where they can both confess their sins. But that would be a serious error. Of course the wife is a sinner too. But whatever sins she may have committed do not justify the husband's abuse, nor should they lessen the need for the church to prioritize addressing that abuse.

It was precisely this mistake that made the reconciliation ministry of Judy Dabler so tragic.[19] As discussed in chapter 1, Dabler was supposed to be a leading authority on biblical conflict resolution. But her reconciliation approach often bypassed the kind of fact-finding that would lead to true accountability and instead started with the assumption that the wrongdoing was equal on both sides. As *Christianity Today* reported, "She did not make it a priority to establish an objective account of the facts . . . even when the conciliation was prompted by allegations of abuse. Advocates for conciliation say the mutual confession of sin is not an appropriate starting point in response to an injustice."[20]

Much more can be said about the proper approach to reconciliation (and we will deal with Matthew 18 in chapter 5). For now, here are several principles to keep in mind as churches seek reconciliation between abusive pastors and their victims.

First, *victims should not be asked to meet with an abusive pastor unless he has been held accountable.* The foundation for reconciliation always begins with the truth about what happened and accountability for what happened. And it is the job of the church, not the victims, to provide that accountability. If the church fails to provide it yet insists the victims meet with the abuser, they have shifted this burden to the victims. The church is making the victims do the job it failed to do. Now the victims are in a position where they have to prove their case, all the while having no protection or help from the church. This scenario provides the abuser more opportunity to attack the victims, essentially abusing them all over again.

Second, *victims should not meet with an abusive pastor unless he is genuinely repentant.* One can imagine a scenario where a church does hold an abusive pastor accountable but that pastor remains defiant and unrepentant. But there can be no biblical reconciliation unless there is real repentance: "If your brother sins, rebuke him, and if he repents, forgive him" (Luke 17:3). In such a scenario, the victims of abuse should wait until an official church body has established that genuine repentance has taken place. It's not enough that the abusive pastor merely *claims* to be repentant. He must demonstrate repentance to a governing body that is able to evaluate it properly.

Third, *victims should not meet with an abusive pastor until they are emotionally and spiritually ready.* Even if the abuser is held accountable and is repentant, that does not mean a reconciliation meeting must take place right away. Many victims of abuse are so deeply traumatized that they struggle to be in the presence of an abuser until real healing has taken place. This may take months, even years.

If victims of abuse refuse to meet, an unrepentant pastor *will likely portray the victims as unforgiving and unwilling to reconcile.* He will take the moral high ground, making himself out to be the peacemaker and the victims as the ones holding a grudge. This is why it is imperative that churches *not even ask* the victims to meet with the abuser until the guidelines are met. That way, the church is preventing the meeting from taking place, not the victims.

A fitting illustration of the danger of peacemaking with an unrepentant abusive leader comes from a scene in J. R. R. Tolkien's *The Two Towers*. After the wizard Saruman's devastating betrayal, he is finally confronted by Gandalf and Theoden, the king of Rohan. Despite the heinous and unspeakable atrocities Saruman commits, he admits no blame and shows no remorse. At the same time—and this is key—he still barters for peace with those he's hurt. He wants what all abusive leaders want: peace without repentance and accountability.

It is remarkable how accurately Tolkien paints the tone and attitude of an abusive leader. When Saruman speaks to Theoden—whom he has sought to destroy, along with Theoden's people—he comes across as kind, reasonable, and peaceable: "Why have you not come before as a friend? Much have I desired to see you."[21] Then he offers peace: "I say, Theoden King: shall we have peace and friendship, you and I? It is ours to command."[22] And when he talks to Gandalf, Saruman invites him up for a peacemaking conversation: "For the common good I am willing to redress the past to receive you. Will you not consult with me? Will you not come up?"[23]

In all these statements—as smooth and charming as they seem—notice there is no admission of guilt or wrongdoing. On the contrary, Saruman does something else abusive leaders do: he portrays himself as the real victim. He flips the script, making himself out to be the grieved party: "Despite the injuries that have been done to me, in which the men of Rohan, alas! have had some part, still I would save you."[24] And when he talks to Gandalf, he doesn't confess his own sins but instead points out Gandalf's sins: "You are proud and do not love advice."[25] In other words, it's everyone else's fault.

Thankfully, despite Saruman's honey-tongued manipulations, Theoden and Gandalf aren't fooled. They don't go up into

Saruman's chambers to broker a peace deal. Theoden is quite plain: "We will have peace, when you and your works have perished. . . . You are a liar, Saruman, and a corrupter of men's hearts."[26] Similarly, Gandalf does not accept the offer to meet: "Nay, I do not think I will come up. But listen, Saruman, for the last time! Will you not come down?"[27] Instead of meeting on Saruman's terms, Gandalf simply calls Saruman to repentance—and does so with genuineness and earnestness. But, like most abusive leaders, Saruman will not relent. Thus, Gandalf removes his office from him: "You have become a fool, Saruman, and yet pitiable. You might have still turned away from folly and evil, and have been of service. But you chose to stay. . . . I cast you from the order and from the Council."[28]

CONCLUSION

When an elder board or Christian organization is faced with accusations that their pastor or leader is abusive, we need to realize they may already have the following assumptions: (1) this is an isolated incident (what dead bodies?); (2) this pastor seems like an honest, good person whom we know and love (there are no monsters); (3) everyone's an awful sinner and blame must exist on all sides (everyone's a monster); and (4) accountability isn't needed because conflicts can be solved if the two parties just meet together (just meet with the monster).

Take these assumptions and add to them the extensive and robust defensive tactics that most abusive pastors employ, and we are faced with a rather concerning implication: *In this current system, it is extremely difficult—indeed almost impossible—to convict a pastor of spiritual abuse.* Unless the case is particularly severe and there is an overwhelming amount of external evidence (videos, recordings, emails), it is unlikely the spiritually abusive pastor will be charged of the testimony of the victims, getting church courts to see the truth is a long, uphill battle.

Clearly there is more work to be done. If we are to battle against abuse in the church, we must understand more than just the theological errors that have allowed it to go unchecked. We must also understand the array of tactics the abuser and his enablers use to defend his abusive actions. We turn to that topic in the next chapter.

FIVE

FLIPPING THE SCRIPT

The Retaliatory Tactics
of Abusive Leaders

> *Evil always wins through the strength*
> *of its splendid dupes; and there has in all*
> *ages been a disastrous alliance between*
> *abnormal innocence and abnormal sin.*
> **—G. K. CHESTERTON**

In April 2018 Bill Hybels, senior pastor of one of the most iconic and successful churches in the United States, Willow Creek Community Church, announced that he would be stepping down after forty-two years in ministry. By many standards, his ministry had been a smashing success. Willow Creek drew nearly twenty-five thousand worshipers each week to the main campus and seven satellite campuses. It was a model to thousands of other churches across the world of how to effectively reach the lost by building a worship experience that was friendly and welcoming to non-Christians. It seemed

Hybels would ride off into the sunset, having accomplished amazing things for the kingdom of God.

Unbeknownst to the congregation at the time, allegations began to surface as far back as 2014 that Hybels, for many years, had engaged in inappropriate sexual relationships with women in his church, including employees. While the elders of the church had conducted their own "investigation" and determined that he had done nothing wrong—Hybels had supposedly been "cleared"[1]—the allegations had not gone away.

So in an apparent effort to get ahead of the story, Hybels finally spoke publicly to the *Chicago Tribune*. According to the *Tribune*, Hybels flatly denied all the charges, claiming that former staff and church members were lying and had inexplicably colluded against him: "This has been a calculated and continual attack on our elders and on me for four long years. . . . I want to speak to all the people around the country that have been misled . . . for the past four years and tell them in my voice, in as strong a voice as you'll allow me to tell it, that the charges against me are false. There still to this day is not evidence of misconduct on my part."[2]

Beyond this statement to the press, Hybels also publicly denied the charges at a "family meeting" with his own congregation—a denial that was met with a standing ovation.[3]

Despite Hybels's attempt to control the narrative, one year later a robust third-party investigation concluded that these women had been telling the truth all along.[4] And it wasn't just sexual abuse that was in play; the report also indicated *spiritual abuse*, as Hybels was said to have a pattern of intimidating and verbally attacking members of the church staff.[5] If anyone disagreed with him, he would "power up."[6] So definitive was the reversal that the entire elder board of Willow Creek eventually resigned as well.[7]

This entire case—as tragic as it is—highlights a sobering reality: abusive leaders employ aggressive and well-orchestrated tactics to keep from being discovered. These tactics are so common in cases across the country that it almost seems as if the abusive pastors are reading from the same playbook. Hybels engaged in some of the most common of these tactics, including profuse denials, rallying a group of defenders, attacking the accusers, and making himself out to be the victim of a conspiratorial plot to ruin his good name. In short, abusive pastors try to defend themselves by "flipping the script." Unfortunately, these tactics work.

The purpose of this chapter is to help churches understand these tactics so they can be identified and addressed. Here are the most common defensive tactics of abusive leaders.

BUILD A COALITION OF DEFENDERS

An abusive pastor's first step is to build a strong coalition of allies who can speak up for him, defend him, and even go on the offensive against the victims. This coalition effectively becomes the abusive pastor's team of lawyers, committed to defending him at all costs.

The building of the coalition doesn't usually begin the moment accusations are made. Most abusive pastors have been doing this for years, forging relationships on the leadership board in case a situation like this might arise. While it's perfectly normal behavior for the senior pastor to have close relationships with other elders, those close relationships are often used as protection from accountability in cases of spiritual abuse. As soon as accusations come to light, the behind-the-scenes networking begins as he weaves his own narrative about what happened. By the time the victims tell their story to a committee, the abusive pastor has already turned most of the elders against them. This is why many victims opt to leave. Since the pastor has controlled the narrative, they realize there's no hope of overcoming the abusive pastor's tactics.

An abuse survivor tells his story:

> At first I tried to confront the abusive person. After that didn't work out, it was too late to share with my friends because he beat me to all of them and told them not to talk to me, to not return my texts, calls, or emails. Since loyalty to him was what he enforced—not even my closest friends would talk to me. I was cut off instantly.[8]

An abusive pastor's ability to build a coalition of defenders goes beyond his personal relationships with these people. It is also because *he is asking them to do something that is more psychologically natural to them.* Generally speaking, people prefer to act as defenders rather than accusers, especially in a Christian context and especially on behalf of a pastor. Thus, most elders or church members quickly become aggressive defenders of a pastor—even lobbying others to join the cause—while very few become advocates for the victims. After all, the latter requires them to accuse the pastor, whom God supposedly called to be a leader. And that is difficult for most people to do. Defending is heroic. Accusing is risky.

This entire scenario reminds us again that the problem with spiritual abuse in the church goes well beyond the individual abusive pastor. Spiritual abuse is allowed to continue because willing supporters protect and enable that pastor.

INSIST PROPER PROCESS WASN'T FOLLOWED

In the 1997 political film *Wag the Dog*, the spin doctor Conrad Brean, played by Robert De Niro, describes the most important factor when controlling a narrative: "To change the story, change the lead."[9] In other words, make the main issue something other than the alleged crime that was committed. This is a move designed to *flip the script*.

For defense attorneys wanting to deflect attention from the guilt of their client, this is critical advice. And one of the most common legal tactics designed to "change the lead" is to file numerous procedural objections: There was no search warrant. No Miranda rights were given. The jury did not receive proper instructions. Before long, the conversation has ceased to be about the crime and is now about the procedure. And that is exactly what the defendant wants.

It is no different in abuse cases in the church. Abusive pastors often deflect the attention off what they've done by issuing loud complaints that proper procedures weren't followed. So loudly do they object that they begin to look like the victims and the abused individuals appear to be the real perpetrators.

In a number of cases I studied, it was not unusual for procedural issues to become so central that the abuse itself was nearly forgotten. People were upset, but not at the pastor's abusive behavior. Instead, they were upset about how certain procedural steps weren't followed during his prosecution. In their minds, it was the abusive pastor who had been mistreated; he was the *real* victim. Often these same people express little concern over how the victims had been treated.

Certainly, an accurate and fair judicial process does matter, just like in the secular courts. In any case where a person is accused, we have to make sure they are treated fairly and impartially. But we should be concerned if procedural issues become so central that the pastoral abuse itself is forgotten.

Of all the procedural objections, one is trumpeted louder than any other: *the victims didn't follow Matthew 18*. So let's address that objection more fully. Here's the passage in full:

> If your brother sins against you, go and tell him his fault, between you and him alone. If he listens to you, you have gained your

brother. But if he does not listen, take one or two others along with you, that every charge may be established by the evidence of two or three witnesses. If he refuses to listen to them, tell it to the church. And if he refuses to listen even to the church, let him be to you as a Gentile and a tax collector. (Matt. 18:15–17)

While Matthew 18 is an important passage for dealing with sins in a congregation, it isn't exhaustive; it is not meant to address or solve every possible scenario. Unfortunately, sometimes it is treated like a universal cure that can be applied to every situation. Here are several important clarifications that prove to be especially relevant to abuse cases.

First, we must remember that Matthew 18 applies only to *individuals who have been sinned against*. It doesn't just say, "If your brother sins," but rather, "If your brother sins *against you*."[10] Thus, the passage doesn't apply to every situation where one person might accuse another of sin. For example, if a member of a church staff has watched a pastor abuse *other* members of the staff, they are not obligated to go to that pastor directly. They can go straight to the elder board and report the bad behavior. In fact, 1 Timothy 5:19—"Do not admit a charge against an elder except on the evidence of two or three witnesses"—implies that such charges against an elder can be brought directly to church leadership.

Abusive pastors are understandably eager to block this sort of complaint from ever making it to the elder board. So the pastor's defenders or the pastor himself will often rebuke the accuser by saying something like, "Why didn't you go to the pastor first as Matthew 18 requires?" The problem is that Matthew 18 doesn't apply in this case.

Notably, just a few verses later, Jesus gives a positive example of direct reporting when one person sins against another: the unmerciful servant mistreating someone who owes him money (Matt. 18:21–35).

When the other servants notice his bad behavior, they don't confront him directly. Instead, the text says, "They went and reported to their master all that had taken place" (v. 31). The master did not say, "Well, have you confronted the unmerciful servant yourself?" No, in this case, the rule does not apply.

Second, even if the accuser should have followed Matthew 18 but failed to do so, that does not mean the elder board or other governing body should overlook the sins of the abusive pastor. Some abusive pastors treat Matthew 18 like Miranda rights—if the technical procedures aren't followed, then they are unable to be prosecuted for the crime. But failing to follow Matthew 18 does not give someone a "get out of jail free card." The church should still hold the pastor accountable for his abusive actions even if the accuser did not follow the right steps. Sure, the accuser's failure to follow Matthew 18 should be addressed too, but there should be no attempt to make the two issues equally problematic, as if failing to follow Matthew 18 is equivalent to being an abusive shepherd.

Third, even if the accuser follows Matthew 18 and the abusive pastor admits some wrongdoing, that does not necessarily mean the behavior should not be reported to the church's leadership. Some pastors *want* their victims to follow Matthew 18 so they can "resolve" the issue through a quick apology and move on without anyone else knowing. In other words, abusive pastors sometimes use Matthew 18 as a method of silencing the victims and keeping their track record of conflict under wraps.

But some behaviors are indeed serious enough that a member is justified in reporting it to the larger leadership body, even if the abusive pastor seems apologetic about it. Certainly, this includes blatant criminal behaviors where law enforcement needs to be involved. But a case can be made that a member could justifiably report spiritually abusive behavior too: verbal attacks, berating or humiliating a church member, threatening to fire an employee, and more. Bringing such behavior to the attention of those who are responsible for the oversight of that pastor's ministry does not violate Matthew 18.

Fourth, some abuse cases are so severe that making the victim confront the abusive pastor privately would be irresponsible. For instance, if a pastor sexually groped a female staff member, it would be, in the words of McKnight and Barringer, "inexcusable and psychologically violent" to insist she meet with the perpetrator one-on-one.[11] Indeed, no godly husband, having found out what happened to his wife, would force her back into a room alone with such a person under the pretenses of Matthew 18.[12] Yet in the case of Bill Hybels, the female victims were scolded for not following Matthew 18 and meeting with Hybels privately.[13]

Could those same concerns apply to certain cases of spiritual abuse? I think so. Again, one could understand how a husband might (rightly) refuse to allow his wife to meet alone with a pastor who has verbally intimidated and attacked her. As Lisa Oakley, an expert in spiritual abuse, has argued regarding Matthew 18, "When we get to a situation of spiritual abuse, there's a mismatch of power. And, actually, trying to get people together in a room at the beginning is not something you would do with other forms of abuse."[14]

While the lines aren't always clear, and there are inevitable gray areas that can be debated, we should remember that Matthew 18 is not a catchall passage that applies to every conceivable scenario.

Here's the point: If a pastor is accused of abusive behavior, be wary if procedural issues become the biggest concern of all those involved.

CLAIM TO BE THE VICTIM OF SLANDER

If a pastor is accused of spiritual abuse, it would not be surprising, nor would it be inappropriate, for him to declare his innocence. He might, in fact, be innocent. But it is wholly different for that pastor to declare that he has been slandered. That is more than a claim of innocence; it is an aggressive countercharge that the accusers themselves are engaged in despicable and sinful behavior. It's a way to present himself as the victim and the accusers as the problem. In other words, it is a methodology designed to *flip the script*.

The counterclaims of slander—or gossip—are all too common in cases of spiritual abuse. Time and again, abusive pastors argue that they are the victims of a conspiratorial plot against them as their enemies have colluded to smear their good name. As noted, Hybels made this very claim in his *Chicago Tribune* interview: "This has been a calculated and continual attack on our elders and on me for four long years."[15] Mike Cosper, in his podcast *The Rise and Fall of Mars Hill*, noticed this same trend: "There's a clear pattern in churches in conflict where leaders who want to quell the conflict address it by calling it all 'gossip' and labelling those who are sharing their stories as 'divisive' or 'wolves.'"[16]

Abusive leaders also use the category of slander to their advantage in another way. Some churches and organizations develop an environment where anyone who speaks negatively about the leader will be accused of slander. In other words, these groups silence people by *threatening* them (either explicitly or implicitly) with potential charges of slander. This aggressive posture creates a ministry culture where people live in fear; if they ever speak up, they will be castigated, charged, or fired. When one of Ravi Zacharias's team members spoke up about Zacharias's troubling behavior, that individual was reprimanded for "spreading rumors."[17]

This fear keeps people quiet. In several spiritual abuse cases I studied, an abusive pastor mistreated staff members—even for many years—yet they never knew that other staff members were experiencing the same treatment. Everyone assumed their situation was an isolated case. The reason for this silence became clear: if they spoke negatively about the senior pastor to another member of staff, they knew they could be accused of slander and probably fired. So, out of fear, they all remained quiet. This allowed the abuse to continue unchecked for years.

How can churches or Christian organizations avoid creating a culture where people are afraid to speak up? First, they need to make sure they have the correct definition of *slander*. While the term is frequently used, it is often misunderstood. Slander is not merely saying something negative about another person. Rather, it is saying something negative *while knowing it is false (or at least having no basis to think it is true)*. In other words, slander involves a malicious intent to harm another person's reputation by spreading lies about them (2 Sam. 10:3; 1 Kings 21:13; Prov. 6:16–19; 16:28; Ps. 50:19–20).[18]

Here we should pause and consider that slander is a very serious sin. To lie about another person is something the Lord hates (Prov. 6:16). Such lies can destroy a person's reputation and ministry. But telling the truth is not slander. To speak up about a pastor's abusive behavior—in appropriate ways—is not slander.

There is a rich irony, then, when the accused pastor offers a strong countercharge of slander. If he has no evidence that the accuser is lying, *then the pastor himself may be guilty of slander*. In other words, the pastor expressing concern over unjust accusations may actually be making an unjust accusation against someone else. And when the pastor's defenders repeat the claim that he is a victim of slander—without any evidence that the accusers have malicious intent—then they too may be guilty of slander.

Now, one might wonder what it means if there is an ecclesiastical investigation and the abusive pastor is acquitted. Does that suddenly make the original charges slanderous? Not at all. We already noted how difficult it can be to convict a pastor of spiritual abuse. All the odds are stacked against it. After all, the initial investigations of Steve Timmis, James MacDonald, and Bill Hybels all resulted in some form of exoneration. So an "acquittal" does not necessarily prove that the original charges were mistaken. It may just mean there wasn't enough explicit evidence or perhaps that the investigative body was unable to condemn one of their own. Either way, if the victim came forward in good faith about their concerns, then no slander was involved.

Just a quick word about gossip, which is a close cousin to slander.[19] The two are similar in that they both involve negative reports. But whereas slander is false, gossip may be true. The problem with gossip is not necessarily that it's false information but that it's information shared with malicious intent—namely, to harm a person's reputation or to entertain or titillate others.

Gossip also is a serious sin that churches should address. But we must remember that not all negative reports are gossip. A person may share a negative report about someone without malicious intent. Indeed, victims of abuse may share their story with others for many *legitimate* reasons: to get advice on how to proceed, to get counseling and encouragement for what they've endured, or to warn others about the pastor's bad behavior. This last reason is particularly noteworthy. One might even say that a church member has a moral obligation to speak up about the pastor's bad behavior to protect other church members from being harmed. Paul seems to act in this way when he warns others about the bad behavior of Alexander the coppersmith: "Beware of him yourself, for he strongly opposed our message" (2 Tim. 4:15).

Second, in addition to understanding the definition of *slander*, churches need to avoid creating a culture of fear around slander by assessing, honestly and fairly, the *likelihood of false accusations of abuse against a pastor*. In some churches, members are viewed with a spirit of suspicion, as if they are always on the verge of lying or making false accusations against the leadership. The biggest fear is not that church members will be abused but that a pastor will be abused.

Thus, when people step forward with concerns, there's a built-in disposition that these folks are probably lying and that the pastor needs to be trusted and defended.

But churches need to consider whether this built-in disposition is justified. Is there an epidemic of false abuse accusations against pastors? Do statistics show that church members are prone to lie about abuse? All the indicators we have suggest that the answer is no. While there are no hard statistics on spiritual abuse accusations, the percentage of false accusations in cases of sexual abuse hovers somewhere between 2 percent and 7 percent.[20] And given that most abuse cases are not reported, the actual percentage is probably lower still. If there is a parallel with spiritual abuse—and the two forms of abuse are often linked—then we have little reason to think false accusations are a statistically significant problem.

Churches also need to consider the *enormous price* people pay when they come forward and speak up about spiritual abuse. Typically, they are not believed, they have their character attacked and tarnished, and are driven out of the churches they love (see chapter 6 for examples). What would motivate them to lie about the charges? What would they have to gain? Often they have everything to lose.

This doesn't mean people never lie about whether pastors are abusive. Of course they do. And when it does happen, it should be taken very, very seriously. But we shouldn't assume an accuser is lying.

Now, one might argue that there are other types of false accusations besides lying. Even if the accusers aren't lying, they might still be *mistaken* about their claims. They might *think* they suffered abuse when they really didn't; they may just have an overly sensitive personality that led them to exaggerate what happened. They just blew it out of proportion.

Fair enough. This important possibility has to be considered and is all the more reason for an independent, third-party investigation (more on that in chapter 7). In the meantime, there is one factor that can help clear up questions about whether an accuser has made a mountain out of a molehill: Has more than one accuser come forward? If multiple people have stepped forward with similar stories and claims, then their credibility goes up considerably. It is hard to imagine that all these people share the same proclivity to exaggerate and see something that isn't there. Is that possible? Sure, it's possible. But is it likely? In most cases, no.

Sadly, even when multiple witnesses come forward, that doesn't necessarily mean they are believed. In numerous cases I studied, multiple witnesses told the same story of bullying and intimidation. Even so, the church's leadership board did not believe these testimonies. These cases demonstrate again how difficult it is to prosecute spiritual abuse.

ATTACK THE CHARACTER OF THE VICTIMS

During Harvey Weinstein's 2020 sexual assault trial, the aggressive tactics of his "rottweiler"[21] lawyer, Donna Rotunno, quickly became the focus of the media reports. Rather than defending Weinstein as a good and decent man who could never have done these things, she adopted an old-school, scorched-earth approach: *destroy the character of the victims.*[22] During the seven-week-long trial, her strategy was to present the victims as opportunistic manipulators who used sex with Weinstein to boost their careers. She cross-examined one poor witness for nine hours, regularly causing her to sob uncontrollably on the stand.

Her message was simple: the witnesses were the real perpetrators, not Weinstein.

This same defensive tactic is one of the most common in spiritual abuse cases. And abusive pastors often have their own team of "lawyers" who are more than willing to go along with it. In case after case, abusive leaders shift the attention to all the character flaws or behavioral problems in their accusers. In other words, it is a tactic designed to *flip the script*. And it works. The reason abuse victims are often scared to come forward is because they've seen what happens to those who do. They can see that those who've spoken up in the past have had their lives destroyed, and they don't want to end up like them.

This character attack on the victims happens in a number of ways. First, the abusive pastor might bring up the *past sins* of the victims. Since everyone is a sinner, it should be no surprise that the victims of abuse sin. And because the abusive pastor has usually had a long relationship with the victims, he is all too familiar with their sin patterns. Beyond this, as noted in chapter 2, abusive churches often pressure their members to openly confess their darkest sins. So the abusive leader is well positioned to retaliate by dredging up all the issues in the lives of the witnesses.

As we also noted in chapter 2, there are reasons to doubt the abusive pastor's claims about the sins of the victims. Often the abusive pastor is wrong about a person's sins, or at least exaggerates them. Regardless, the tactic still works. For fear of having their own sins put on display, many victims avoid coming forward at all. Usually, they just leave the church, hoping to avoid the embarrassment that could be caused by the retaliatory wrath of an angry senior pastor.

Second, in addition to highlighting past sins, the abusive pastor might attack *the way the victims are handling the conflict*. He might weave a narrative that paints the victims as unforgiving, angry, hard-hearted, and unwilling to reconcile, all while painting himself as a peacemaker who has reached out with an olive branch that has been repeatedly rejected.

Several factors are overlooked in such a narrative. For one, when people are mistreated and abused, they may lash out or be angry. Yes, this behavior is sinful, but that does not negate the pastor's abuse or absolve him of blame. If a bully picks on a kid at school for months and months and that kid eventually retaliates, the blame for the whole affair doesn't suddenly shift. The bully is still responsible for the months of abusive behavior.

Here is where the church needs to be very careful. Because of what the victim has been through, it is often the case that "the victim appears uncooperative, mistrusting, fearful, angry and hard-hearted."[23] Meanwhile, the abusive leader, at least outwardly, often appears to be cooperative and conciliatory as he engages with the process. Indeed, "He seems to get it and is working hard to change."[24] The danger here is that it can begin to look like the abuser is the good guy and the victim is the bad guy. And this often leads to a tragic result, "church support and pastoral care rallies around the abuser who [appears to be] working so hard to reconcile."[25]

But prior studies on abuse have shown that this outward perception of the abuser and the victim is only that—an outward perception.[26] Once the abusive leader is confronted over his sinful actions and called to repentance, it is often the case that his cooperative spirit will quickly disappear and he will begin to lash out at those holding him accountable. Moreover, as the victims are given time and space to heal and recover, it is often the case that their defensive walls come down and they begin to trust again.

In other words, the abusive leader is happy to offer an olive branch as long as he never has to admit any real wrongdoing. Like Saruman in *The Lord of the Rings*, he won't repent of his actions but still insists on brokering "peace" with the victims. As noted in the prior chapter, this allows him to look like the better man who's wanting to reconcile, while never owning the deep damage he's done.

Third, sometimes victims are accused of having a *victimhood mentality.* In a number of testimonies I read, the victims were portrayed as too easily offended and bothered by the legitimate expressions of pastoral authority. This type of claim will play well in certain churches that are irritated at what they see as the victimhood mentality prevalent in our broader culture.[27] For these churches, the problem isn't the bully pastor but the "progressive" church members who are overly sensitive.

Closely related to this sort of tactic is the additional claim that you can't trust the testimony of these victims because their experience probably clouds their judgment. They're just too close to it all, it is argued. They're overly emotional and therefore unreliable. This tactic is often used if the victim coming forward is a woman. It's all too easy for an abusive pastor to convince a room of his fellow, all-male elders that a woman cannot be trusted because she, like all women, is too sensitive and therefore unreliable (unlike him, of course).

Aside from the profound lack of charity and compassion in such a response, not to mention the demeaning way it portrays women, it also has logical flaws. For one, why is it that victims of abuse are the only ones whose personal experience affects their judgment? Does the personal experience of church elders not affect *their* judgment? Couldn't a positive personal church experience make it harder to spot abuse? Or lead one to believe it is exceptionally unlikely? And couldn't their friendship with the senior pastor also affect their judgment?

Also, we would never apply this argument to other spheres of life. What if we discounted the incredible testimony of Harriet Tubman about the horrific abuse she and others suffered as slaves because we insisted that her experience must have clouded her judgment? Would we really suggest she was prone to exaggeration because she was too close to it all and therefore overly emotional— probably because she was a woman? I hope not.

Fourth, it is not unusual for an abusive pastor to fabricate claims against the victims to make himself look better. In testimonies I read from a church in the Southwest, an abusive pastor, to defend himself from an investigation, spread lies against an elder and his wife, telling members that they were trying to run him off so their son could become the new pastor. There was no evidence for such claims; they were completely fabricated. I wish such outright lies in abuse cases were rare, but I have seen this behavior in story after story.

These tactics to malign the character of the victims are deeply disturbing. But they are used because they work. The tragedy is that some churches have allowed these sorts of counteraccusations to be leveled against abuse victims, leaving them exposed and unprotected. That should occasion some serious soul-searching for anyone in Christian leadership.

TOUT YOUR OWN CHARACTER AND ACCOMPLISHMENTS

Not only is the abusive leader quite willing to attack the character of the victims, but he also attempts to bolster his own character and accomplishments. At this point, appeals are made to everything this individual has done to bless the church: he has labored faithfully for twenty years, he has planted many other churches, he has mentored countless young pastors, he has been a faithful member of his denomination, and more. In short, abusive pastors want to put their (carefully edited) résumé on display.

One feature of this tactic is for the abusive pastor to get character references. He or his supporters might organize a campaign to collect written statements from all sorts of people he's blessed over the years, explaining what a wonderful, kind, and generous pastor he has been—how he helped them through a tough time, gave them good advice, or was a particularly caring shepherd.

All this evidence is designed to create cognitive dissonance in the minds of the elder board or other adjudicating body. How can a man who's accomplished so much good for the kingdom, or who's helped so many people, be the same kind of man who would mistreat and bully members of his church? To resolve this cognitive dissonance, people default to assuming the charges can't possibly be true. This is another way abusive pastors *flip the script*. They convince people that they, not the victims, are the trustworthy ones.

Most churches don't realize that ministry accomplishments and character references *are not determining factors in whether a pastor is abusive*. Virtually any Christian leader who's been in ministry for a decent length of time could trumpet his accomplishments and find people who've been blessed by his ministry. Indeed, how many local pastors could go toe to toe with the accomplishments of someone like Ravi Zacharias? Or Bill Hybels? Or Mark Driscoll? And yet they were all perpetrators of abuse.

As noted in chapter 4, abusive pastors have two sides. One side is often warm, caring, and endearing. The other is harsh, cold, and cruel. Most people have seen only the good side of the abusive pastor. So it would not at all be surprising that such an individual might have a plentiful supply of character references. But this does not mean he is not abusive.

PLAY THE SYMPATHY CARD

Even though the victims of spiritual abuse have suffered greatly (more on this topic in the next chapter), one tactic of abusive leaders is to talk about how much *they've* suffered. They will go to great lengths to describe how much pain they are in because of the unresolved "conflict" with those accusing them. They will tell how they have lost sleep, been wracked with anxiety, and are "deeply saddened" by the whole affair.[28] Even Saruman wanted to talk about the "injuries that have been done to me."[29] This move is designed to engender sympathy not for the victims but for the abuser. Again, it is designed to *flip the script.*

To produce even more sympathy, some abusive leaders then appeal to how the whole situation has affected their spouse or their family. They might point out how much their wife has suffered or how their kids are heartbroken and disillusioned.[30] This tactic is effective precisely because we *ought* to feel sympathy for the family members harmed by the scandal. Often the spouses and children are unaware of how the pastor has mistreated others (though some spouses enable and defend their husband's abusive behavior and sometimes even participate in his deceptions). Indeed, some church courts feel less inclined to prosecute such a pastor because they feel sorry for his family, which "has suffered enough."

But sympathy for the family should not lessen the need to hold the abusive pastor accountable. It is *his* behavior, not that of the victims, that brought pain to his own family. Instead of blaming others, he should take responsibility for his own actions.

CONCLUSION

As varied as spiritual abuse cases can be, abusive leaders often follow the same well-organized playbook to defend themselves. The purpose of this chapter has been to describe and respond to each step in that playbook so that churches are better equipped to protect their congregations, particularly the victims who have the courage to step forward and tell their stories.

Unfortunately, not all churches understand the tactics we discussed, and therefore many victims remain unprotected. Not only are they abused by their pastors, but then, in turn, they are not believed or protected by their churches. They are abused twice, often with tragic effects. The next chapter will explore those varied effects so churches can better appreciate the damage that can be done if they fail to hold abusive pastors accountable.

SIX

SUFFERING IN SILENCE

The Devastating Effects of Spiritual Abuse

There are some wounds that
cannot be wholly cured.
—GANDALF

J. R. R. Tolkien's epic tale, *The Lord of the Rings,* doesn't end like most adventure novels. While Sauron and the forces of darkness are ultimately defeated, and while there is great joy and celebration over the victory, Tolkien is more honest than most about the ongoing effects of deep, sustained conflict. Frodo, the protagonist and hero, does not—as we might have hoped and expected—live happily ever after. Even though he returns to the Shire and to his beloved Bag End, Frodo knows he will never be the same: "How do you go on when in your heart you begin to understand . . . there is no going back? There are some things that time cannot mend. Some hurts that go too deep."[1]

Then, in a conversation with his companion Sam, Frodo realizes that all his pain may not be about saving the Shire for himself but saving it for others. Their exchange is deeply moving:

> "But," said Sam, and tears started in his eyes, "I thought you were going to enjoy the Shire, too, for years and years, after all you have done."
>
> "So, I thought too, once" [said Frodo]. "But I have been too deeply hurt, Sam. I tried to save the Shire, and it has been saved, but not for me. It must often be so, Sam, when things are in danger: someone has to give them up, lose them, so others may keep them."[2]

Those affected by spiritual abuse feel much as Frodo did. Though they try to put their old life back together, they realize things will never be the same. Some wounds go too deep. Often their one consolation, like Frodo, is that their courage to speak may have protected and saved others. Though they may never experience the beauty of church again in the same way, perhaps their actions have preserved the church so others can.

Unfortunately, some churches have minimized the problem, unaware of how deep these wounds run, sometimes even insisting that victims should just "get over it" and move on with their lives. The purpose of this chapter is to push back against this misconception by exploring these wounds of spiritual abuse more fully. If churches are to be motivated to act—to proactively guard against abusive pastors—they have to come face-to-face with the devastating effects of spiritual abuse.

EMOTIONAL EFFECTS

We begin with the most obvious effects of spiritual abuse—namely, that it wreaks havoc on the emotional state of the abused. Studies have shown that victims struggle with a number of emotions for years, maybe even for the rest of their lives.

FEAR. This is one of the most dominant emotions for those who've endured abuse.[3] It can be debilitating and crippling in extreme cases. Victims fear many outcomes: retaliation from the abusive pastor, the ruining of their reputation, the loss of their job and livelihood, the alienation of their friends and their church. Some also fear making mistakes in the complicated judicial process that often surrounds abuse cases. For example, they might wonder, "Who am I allowed to talk to? What steps should I take? What if I trust someone who then turns against me?" And many fear the future: "Will I ever recover from the pain? Will my life ever be the same?"

Fear is one of the most potent weapons in the hands of an abusive pastor. Members of the church are often afraid to speak out because they know what happens to those who do. Each destroyed life the abusive pastor leaves behind is a warning sign to those who remain in the church.

ANGER. This is a close cousin of fear. For many, the latter naturally leads to the former. Spiritual abuse victims often report deep-seated anger that they have never experienced before. The anger can be aimed in many directions: anger at the abuser for his treatment of them, anger at the church leadership for its failure to protect them, anger at friends who have betrayed them, anger about the lies and disparaging remarks that have been made about them, and anger at the lack of justice and accountability. In addition, there is often anger toward God (Why didn't you stop this abuse? Why haven't you held the abusive pastor accountable?) or even anger toward themselves (Why did I let this happen? Why didn't I see this coming?).

SHAME. Like victims of other types of abuse (physical, sexual), spiritual abuse victims also feel great shame.[4] This is paradoxical emotion because the victims are not to blame for what happened to them. But the shame still affects the victims for two reasons. First, victims wonder whether this whole thing may somehow be their fault. Since the abusive leader has been gaslighting them with accusations—you're insubordinate, you're a difficult person, you're the problem—the victims sometimes wonder whether those claims are true. Tragically, victims often struggle to get the words of the abusive pastor out of their heads.

Second, some level of shame flows from wondering what others now think about them. Since the abusive pastor and his "lawyers" often tarnish their reputations, the victims feel like they are the guilty party *in other people's eyes.* As they interact with others, they constantly wonder, "What does this person think about me? Does this person think I am to blame?" Insecurity about what other people think provides a perpetual feeling of shame even if they know they are innocent.

DEPRESSION. The combination of fear, anger, and shame often leads to depression in the abused.[5] Because of what happened to them, they may feel like life is meaningless, that there is no justice, and that there's no reason to live life like they once did. They battle low energy; lack of motivation; and bouts of despair, hopelessness, and a general lack of interest in the activities they once enjoyed. This sort of depression has physical and spiritual manifestations, both of which we will discuss in the next sections.

POST-TRAUMATIC STRESS DISORDER. PTSD is not uncommon in cases of spiritual abuse. After fearful, dangerous, or traumatic events, people often suffer for months (even years) with the after-effects of those events, including upsetting memories, fear, sadness, nervousness, and bursts of anxiety.[6] In short, "people who have PTSD may feel stressed or frightened even when they're no longer in danger."[7] For spiritual abuse survivors, experiences that remind them of their abusive pastor or church situation usually trigger these effects. These triggers could be something as simple as going to church, hearing a sermon, or seeing individuals from their former church.

A complicating factor in spiritual abuse cases is that the abuse is perpetrated by an institution or a person the victim knew and trusted, known as "institutional betrayal."[8] Studies have shown that abuse within a trusted relationship is significantly more traumatic than abuse by a stranger. And there is a natural trust that is fostered between a church member and their pastor (and the larger leadership body). Smith and Freyd show that such betrayal has a substantial emotional impact: "Betrayal trauma is associated with higher rates of a host of outcomes, including posttraumatic stress disorder (PTSD), dissociation, anxiety, [and] depression."[9]

PHYSICAL EFFECTS

Bessel van der Kolk's 2014 bestseller, *The Body Keeps the Score*, is a fascinating journey into the relationship between trauma and its manifestations in the human body.[10] At the moment the trauma occurs—whether it be a car accident, physical assault, or spiritual abuse—the brain sends out a burst of adrenaline to help the victim deal with that trauma, usually by "flight" or "fight."[11] A rush of adrenaline has predictable physiological results: increased heart rate, rise in blood pressure, and tensing of the muscles.

In a normal situation, those physiological effects dissipate when the threat is past. The problem for some victims of trauma is that the physiological results continue long after the threat is gone. The adrenaline keeps pumping. And this can have serious health consequences: "The stress hormones of traumatized people, in contrast, take much longer to return to baseline and spike quickly and disproportionately in response to mildly stressful stimuli. The insidious effects of constantly elevated stress hormones include memory attention problems, irritability, and sleep disorders. They also contribute to many long-term health issues, depending on which body system is most vulnerable in a particular individual."[12]

Van der Kolk goes on to make another critical observation. If the initial traumatic event was one that the victim was *unable to escape from*—that is, an event where they were "held down, trapped, or otherwise prevented from taking effective action"[13]—then that traumatic event is more prone "to leave long-lasting scars."[14] Why? Because the traumatic event is effectively prolonged, allowing the continued secretion of "stress chemicals," and "the brain's electrical circuits continue to fire in vain."[15] Victims who suffer this sort of trauma are therefore likely to have more long-term physiological effects.

Here we can see how spiritual abuse can be particularly damaging. Unlike the trauma of something one can run away from, spiritual abuse often makes the victims feel trapped and immobilized, with no course of action to protect themselves, their families, and their livelihoods. If we apply the words of Van der Kolk, they are "prevented from taking effective action." Not only does spiritual abuse often occur over long periods of time, but even when it comes to light, the victims are often trapped in a long process (usually years) of litigation and judicial wrangling with the abusive pastor and the church's leadership. This process effectively prolongs the abuse. In this way, the trauma of spiritual and emotional abuse can be similar to the trauma of physical or sexual abuse. Van der Kolk observes, "Emotional abuse and neglect can be just as devastating as physical abuse and sexual molestation."[16]

In sum, *spiritual abuse is prone to create deep and serious mental scars that in turn can produce long-term physiological consequences.*

When we look at cases of spiritual abuse, we see this truth played out. Abuse victims often suffer from a number of physical ailments consistent with PTSD: insomnia, high blood pressure, chronic fatigue, tremors, heart problems, joint and muscle pain, and even auto-immune disorders.[17]

RELATIONAL EFFECTS

Although the emotional and physical impacts of spiritual abuse are painful enough, the *relational* trauma can be particularly severe. Survivors of spiritual abuse testify to having countless relationships destroyed by the behavior of the abusive pastor, who is sometimes enabled by a willing group of supporters and protectors. He accomplishes this destruction by using the retaliatory tactics discussed in chapter 5. These relational rifts are often so severe that most are never healed.

The most obvious damage is that victims are often driven out of their own churches, thereby losing their core relational networks and the ministries they worked hard to build. Recall the case of Paul Petry, one of the pastors at Mars Hill who stood up to Mark Driscoll and was subsequently fired and brought under church discipline. According to the Seattle-based publication the *Stranger*, "Driscoll called on Mars Hill's congregation to shun the Petry family, cutting the parents and children off from all their friends in the church community they'd spent the past several years helping to build."[18] Social ostracization of abuse victims also happened at Steve Timmis's church, the Crowded House. As reported in *Christianity Today*, "To go from being inside a highly relational, tight community to being considered an 'ungospeled' and rebellious outsider can be traumatic."[19] For the "refugees" forced out of the church, it was so awkward to see current church members around town—who they had once been close to—that one ex-member said it might have been easier just to leave the country.

The trauma of this sort of social ostracization is bigger than just the victims missing their former church. It involves the reality that their former church has now been *turned against them* and now regards them as divisive, troublesome, and slanderous. In other words, it's the reversal—moving from faithful member to shunned exile—that is particularly devastating. As one abuse survivor testified, "The emotions of anger, guilt, shame, and a feeling of grief and loss of friendships and of the 'family' network can seem overwhelming, and in many cases, it seems there is nowhere to turn. Friends are silent. The group network has gone. Word spreads quickly into other spiritual circles; will they be considered a troublemaker, or just 'in need' of healing? Will they be believed?"[20]

Victims of the abuse walk around in shame not because they've done anything wrong but because their former church thinks they have. They feel they are "damaged goods."[21]

It gets worse. Beyond the fact that the victims are shunned, they are also forced to watch as other people stay at the church and continue to support the abusive leader(s). Those who remain listen to him preach, shake his hand after the service, and continue to pay their tithe money—acts that serve to legitimize the abusive leader as if nothing were wrong.

These folks who stay behind often defend their decision under the heading that they are neutral and don't want to "take sides." But by staying at the church, they are not neutral. They have clearly chosen a side. Wade Mullen explains how painful this is to the victims: "Consider what it communicates to the watching victims when they see people gathering around the people who wounded them—to see them giving money to the institution, using their services, applauding their efforts, and endorsing their legitimacy."[22]

Thus, he concludes, "Sometimes supporting the victim means immediately withdrawing support from those who have yet to speak the truth about the abuse and refuse to let the light shine."[23]

One tragic aspect of this social ostracization is that it happens precisely when the victims of abuse most need encouragement and support from the body of Christ. Instead, suffering is heaped upon suffering: the victims of abuse are already suffering from the abusive behavior itself, and now the very community that could help them heal from that abuse has been taken away from them also. Thus, they often find themselves suffering in silence, utterly alone.

On top of losing their church, abuse victims often testify that they have also lost some of their closest friends. As Proverbs 16:28 says, "A dishonest man spreads strife, and a whisperer separates close friends." Remember, abusive pastors are good at flipping the script, attacking the character of the victims and making them out to be slanderous and divisive. So even close friends of the victims feel the need to choose sides, often landing on the side of the pastor. One victim of spiritual abuse described this intense relational pain: "Individually and as a family, we lost friendships that we never envisioned we would lose. Our kids lost all their adult mentors. . . . Our family was completely discarded based on whatever the pastor proclaimed . . . It's one thing to endure all of this as a person, or couple, but to have watched the devastation on our kids as well as losing some of our closest friends has probably been the most painful."[24]

Another testimony is equally tragic: "Some of our closest friends didn't want to hear our story, stayed at the church, and eventually aligned against us. The church as a whole shunned us and we lost many people in friendships/community as well as our reputation that had been built over almost 20 years. The pastor's word always prevailed."[25]

I could offer more examples, but these testimonies are sufficient to show how long and wide an abusive pastor's "relational debris field" can be. A single abusive pastor who refuses to repent can destroy countless relationships, tearing a massive rift between friends, elder boards, churches, and communities. If only he had repented, all that relational damage could have been avoided. No wonder God is markedly against abusive shepherds—they have essentially devoured God's own people (Ezek. 34:10).

SPIRITUAL EFFECTS

We close this chapter by examining perhaps the most damaging effects that spiritual abuse has on victims: it often crushes a person's spiritual life and calls into question all they believe. This is why spiritual abuse is a unique kind of abuse. It is perpetrated by God's appointed leader (a pastor), for God's appointed ends (church planting, spreading the gospel), often enabled by God's appointed institution (the church and its elders), and leveled against God's own people (church members). The spiritual damage can be enormous.

DOUBTS ABOUT THE CHURCH. One of the most common sentiments for those who have been spiritually abused is, "I will never go to church again." Indeed, many abuse survivors stay away from the church for long periods of time, and some never return. The reasons for this absence aren't difficult to see. Church activities often trigger bursts of anxiety or emotional pain as survivors are reminded of what they endured in their last church. Just seeing a pastor preach or being in a congregation on a Sunday morning can dredge up hurtful memories. Even hearing a certain passage of Scripture can be painful if the abusive pastor used it to bully and manipulate. In one case I studied, the abuse victim happened to visit a church on a Sunday when they were installing new elders and calling the congregation to submit to their authority. After what she had endured at the hands of her prior elders, it led to a panic attack.

In short, the spiritual abuser takes aspects of church life that are inherently good—preaching, Scripture reading, worship—and makes them a source of pain. This doesn't mean these parts of church life should be abandoned. But it often takes victims a long time to overcome these negative associations.

The other reason abuse victims stay away from the church comes down to an issue of trust.[26] They don't feel safe in any congregation, wondering if that church will someday turn against them too. Consequently, those who have suffered spiritual abuse often find that they are suspicious, worried, and even paranoid about forging new relationships. This makes it difficult for abused people to make friends in their new church—after all, their close friends turned against them at their prior church. Therefore, abuse survivors often find themselves isolated for years as they struggle to build a new community that they feel is safe.

DOUBTS ABOUT CHRISTIANITY. These doubts about the church are closely related to doubts about Christianity itself. Victims of spiritual abuse often testify to how they struggle to believe what they once did.[27] Even if they know that their abusive church doesn't necessarily represent the Christian faith, it can be difficult to separate the two. Consequently, it is natural to ask tough theological questions: Why would God allow abuse like this to happen inside his church? If Christianity is true, then why do churches and pastors behave so cruelly? If the Spirit is at work in the church, then why didn't the elders see the abusive pastor for what he was? If Christian leaders are corrupt, does that mean Christianity is no different from any other religion? Or is Christianity even worse?

Sometimes the questions are less about Christianity and more about the *version* of Christianity in which the abuse happened. The victim may wonder whether a particular denomination systemically tolerates abuse or whether certain theological systems are more prone to allow abusive pastors to take hold. In such cases, the victim may not be inclined to abandon Christianity altogether but the particular stripe of Christianity that they belonged to.

Either way, abuse often leads to great spiritual doubt or spiritual malaise. One survivor said, "I don't have a passion for doing ministry anymore. I don't get excited about anything spiritual anymore."[28] And some abuse victims end up leaving the Christian faith entirely.

DOUBTS ABOUT GOD. Even for those who don't doubt the truth of the Christian faith, spiritual abuse can have another adverse effect: it can distort people's image of what God is like.[29] Because of the toxic behavior of an abusive pastor, a Christian might think God himself must be that way. They may think God is never satisfied with them and is perpetually looking for failure and eager to punish and humiliate them if they stumble. This negative (and unbiblical) view of God can have deleterious spiritual effects.

DOUBTS ABOUT ONESELF. For many spiritual abuse victims, their experience also challenges the way they view themselves. While they may have had a confident Christian identity before the abuse, all that is now called into question. They may wonder, "Who am I really?" One abuse victim said, "I am not the same person and I don't think I ever will be."[30] Part of this identity crisis is related to the victim's changed role in the church. Since people often build their Christian identities around the ministries they serve, that identity can quickly change if those ministries are stripped away. Some victims are forced to rethink their calling and vocation entirely, perhaps for the first time.

Another part of this identity crisis is driven by the victim's doubts about their own character and judgment. If they have been repeatedly gaslighted and told that everything is their fault, a side of them may still wonder if it's true. Victims of abuse repeatedly confess to wondering whether they are going crazy or losing their minds. In addition, victims also have renewed doubts about their own judgment. If they trusted someone they should not have trusted, they may wonder whether they can even trust themselves. Of course, this is a paralyzing combination—trusting neither others nor oneself—that drives the victim further into spiritual, relational, and emotional isolation.

The enormous self-doubt the victims have suffered under is often revealed when someone from the outside confirms their story. One member of Steve Timmis's church reported the relief she felt when the *Christianity Today* article broke: "I read the article and collapsed in a heap on the floor, crying. Nothing in the article surprised me. My main feeling was: 'Oh, I'm not crazy after all!' After 20 years of doubting myself and wondering whether anything had happened or whether it was just me there was a feeling of relief."[31]

CONCLUSION

Anyone who thinks spiritual abuse is a minor problem has not reckoned with the documented devastation. My prayer is that you—especially if you are a pastor or Christian leader of some sort—would let the testimonies in this chapter sink in. Once you let them in, several responses should follow.

First, we should "weep with those who weep" (Rom. 12:15). We must remember that these people are Christ's sheep, our brothers and sisters in Christ. As they suffer deeply and profoundly—some of them even questioning their faith—we are called to show them compassion and care. Sadly, compassion is rare in spiritual abuse cases, at least in the ones I've studied. Instead of having compassion, many churches first ask whether there is a "valid" reason for their suffering. In other words, the first instinct is to *question* and *challenge* the victims instead of offering them Christlike sympathy.

No one is suggesting that people's experiences are automatically self-validating and beyond questioning. There may be a time and a place to probe deeper into whether they are seeing the situation clearly. But surely that should not be the *first* instinct when we are faced with a suffering believer. When a child comes crying to his mother with a skinned knee, the mother's first step is not to interrogate the child about whether he was running too fast on the playground. After all, the suffering itself is real, regardless of the cause, and deserves tenderness and care.

Second, the type of spiritual damage discussed before should cause deep and sober self-reflection in anyone who is called to the pastoral ministry. That a pastor's words and actions could leave such damage should give anyone pause. Jesus gave serious warnings to anyone who might lead others spiritually astray: "It would be better for him if a millstone were hung around his neck and he were cast into the sea" (Luke 17:2). And certainly, that same warning should also apply to other church leaders or elder boards who defend and prop up abusive leaders.

Third, and perhaps most importantly, the content of this chapter ought to motivate us to prevent spiritual abuse whenever possible. Steps must be taken to protect the church from abusive leaders. And so we turn now to the final chapter, where we explore what some of those steps might be.

SEVEN

THEY SHALL NOT HURT OR DESTROY

Creating a Culture That Resists Spiritual Abuse

The scandal is perpetrated in the holy names of Christ and St. Peter. Who can go on tolerating it or keeping silence?
—MARTIN LUTHER

In 1510 Martin Luther—at the time a devoted Augustinian monk— had a remarkable and privileged opportunity. He had the chance to visit the "Eternal City," the glorious capital of not only the empire but of the church: Rome. As the spiritual center of the world, Rome was the place to draw near to God. There were the stored holy relics; there were the bodies of many saints, including Peter and Paul; and there were the church's greatest leaders, including his holy eminence himself, Pope Julius II.

But when Luther visited Rome, his high expectations were shattered. Rather than a glorious city, he found a filthy one, not just physically but spiritually. It was the church leadership that was the problem. Many of the priests were openly corrupt, expressing their outright disbelief in the validity of the Mass and known to engage in sexual immorality with prostitutes. Eventually, Luther called Rome a "den of iniquity."[1]

Luther's experience in Rome played a significant role in his passion to see the church reformed. It was not just the church's doctrinal problems that concerned Luther but also its *moral* problems—especially among the clergy. The church's biggest challenge wasn't a secular world attacking it from the outside, but rather moral corruption arising from the inside. Thankfully, Luther had the courage to stand up and call out the church's wayward leadership. Though he was accused of being divisive and disruptive, he was doing what prophets have done throughout the ages: calling God's people to repentance.

While the state of the church's leadership is much improved since Luther's day, there is a need in every generation to recognize what areas still need growth and to call the church to change. I have argued throughout this volume that one of those areas (though not the only one) is the all-too-prevalent bully pastor. In many places, we have forgotten the biblical paradigm of humble, servant leadership and instead have attracted narcissists who abuse the very flocks they are supposed to protect.

The purpose of this chapter is to lay out some small (in the scope of things, tiny) structural steps that can help the church make some needed changes. It is not intended to unpack all relevant aspects of ecclesiology, polity, or church discipline. Those categories have been ably addressed in other places, and there is not space to explore them here. Rather, I am offering some modest structural changes that will hopefully supplement and round out these categories and perhaps fill in some blind spots.

Structural issues are only one part of a church culture. There's much more that could be said. But, hopefully, it's a place to start.

PREVENTION: KEEPING ABUSIVE LEADERS FROM GAINING A POSITION OF POWER

The best way to stop abusive pastors is never to let them achieve positions of power in the first place. Benjamin Franklin was right: "An ounce of prevention is worth a pound of cure."[2] Thus, the church needs to rethink the way it attracts and recruits pastoral candidates so potentially abusive leaders are weeded out from the start. This process begins with a radical reworking of the job profile for the average senior pastor position or equivalent leadership role. Perhaps we've been attracting the wrong kind of candidates because we've been *looking* for them. Here are a few points to consider for pastoral search committees.

CHARACTER OVER COMPETENCY. When churches put together a candidate profile, they need to begin by laying out a vision for what they think a senior pastor ought to be. By walking through the key texts on Christian leadership (as we did in chapter 3), they can show that they are committed to a leader who is not a bully but gentle (1 Tim. 3:3; cf. Titus 1:7); not out for shameful gain but eagerly serving (1 Peter 5:2); not domineering but setting an example (1 Peter 5:3); and not quarrelsome but kind (2 Tim. 2:24).

To be sure, this doesn't mean the search committee cares *only* about character. Competency in a number of areas matters too. But the church needs to be clear that giftedness is not the only—or main—thing they are looking for.

This candidate profile will clarify the search process because leaders prone to spiritual abuse love to talk about their competencies—what they're good at and what they've accomplished. After all, these leaders are usually quite convinced of their own greatness already and would never miss an opportunity to explore it further with the search committee. They might also want to talk about their doctrinal positions, philosophy of ministry, or approach to preaching. But they aren't so keen to talk about their character, especially if they are expected to embody gentleness, humility, and a servant's heart.

Here's the point: If we create a pastoral profile guided by biblical principles rather than worldly ones, it will hopefully be unattractive to potentially abusive pastors. The key issue is not only whether the church is attracted to the prospective pastor but also whether *the prospective pastor is attracted to this kind of church*. The latter is as important as the former when it comes to weeding out the bad apples. If potentially abusive pastors don't like what they see and remove themselves from the search process voluntarily, all the better.

Of course, the lingering question is how a search committee can get an accurate sense of a candidate's character. Here we have to recognize the (all too obvious) limits of our current system, where candidates are simply asked to provide a few references. While references have some value, everyone knows they are the handpicked friends of the candidate and therefore unlikely to produce a critical appraisal of that candidate's character. Except in rare cases, the references inevitably offer a glowing appraisal of the person under review.

To peel back the layers of a candidate's character, I suggest some additional steps:

- Ask for permission to contact those who worked under the candidate in their prior two jobs. This would include assistant pastors, administrative assistants, ministry coordinators, and more. These individuals, if allowed to speak confidentially, would give significantly more accurate information about the candidate's character.

- Make sure to reach out to *women* at the candidate's prior church, either a volunteer leader or female staff. In my experience, search committees almost never talk to women but only men—and only men handpicked by the candidate. That is a broken system. Women often have a radically different perspective on their church than the men do.

- Ask for permission to speak to the elders of the candidate's prior church, and not just the ones the candidate handpicks. Their evaluation of the pastor after his departure (confidentially, of course) would be enlightening.

- Ask the candidate to talk about any conflicts he's had in ministry over the years and how those were resolved. Probe deeply about whether there are unresolved conflicts where he remains estranged from others in ministry. If the candidate casts himself as the hero in every story of conflict and everyone else is to blame because they wouldn't submit to his authority, those are red flags. As noted in chapter 4, a "trail of dead bodies" is typically a sign of an abusive leader.

A candidate might refuse to allow these steps. But that itself might be a red flag and perhaps a reason to move on to a different candidate. Some may wonder whether such a rigorous probe into a person's character is unfair. After all, wouldn't anyone serving in ministry for any length of time have people who don't like them? And wouldn't such a process uncover a substantial number of negative things? Perhaps. But that doesn't make the process unfair. Instead, it should give the search committee a more sober and realistic sense that whomever they hire will have weaknesses that need to be carefully addressed.

That result would be substantively better than the current

system where the search committee pretends they've found a nearly flawless candidate (even though deep down they know that can't possibly be true) and presents the candidate to the church as such. That scenario—naively putting the new pastor on a pedestal—not only creates an environment ripe for abuse because no one feels the need to hold such a "perfect" candidate accountable but also leads to inevitable disillusionment when they realize he's not perfect.

TEAMWORK OVER HIERARCHY. The pastoral profile should include another desirable characteristic: a pastor who emphasizes team building and cooperation rather than one who executes his ministry in a top-down, hierarchical fashion. In other words, the search committee should make it clear that they want a pastor who leads by consensus and by example, not by command or by coercion (1 Peter 5:3). Keep in mind that many abusive leaders take positions because of the power and control they afford. They want to know in advance that they will be the one in charge, that they will call the shots, somewhat like a head football coach who makes the big decisions and hires and fires whomever he pleases. Sure, they may give lip service to a plurality of elders and mutual submission to the brethren. But at the end of the day, they just want to be in control. Once they realize this job affords no such power, they may look elsewhere.

ACCOUNTABILITY OVER SECRECY. Finally, the pastoral profile should indicate that there will be a substantive accountability plan for the pastor. I will talk more about particular structural and procedural suggestions, but the church should make it clear that they will have a transparent system where people can share their concerns about the senior pastor without being silenced, blacklisted, or isolated as a result. The church needs to state that it wants to avoid a culture of fear where people are afraid to speak and instead values a culture where all voices are heard, respected, and valued—even, and perhaps especially, if they are critical of the church leadership.

Churches need to be careful that an accountability system is not misused in a way that *encourages* criticism of the pastor. The goal is not to stir up complaints and grievances. After all, there's never a shortage of those. Rather, the goal is to create a safe space for concerns to be raised so there isn't undue retaliation and targeting of those bringing the concerns.

ACCOUNTABILITY: OVERSEEING CHURCH LEADERS ONCE THEY'RE IN A POSITION OF POWER

Once a pastor is hired, there has to be a process by which they are given the proper oversight and shepherding. Case after case of spiritual abuse has shown that it was the lack of any real accountability that allowed the pastor to gain a disproportionate amount of power and then to abuse that power with little or no consequences. Given space limitations, we can only begin a conversation on these matters here. And since polity rules vary widely in different denominations, the following suggestions don't necessarily fit with every denomination. You will have to determine which structural changes fit your particular context.

LIMITING POWER. We begin with the most obvious consideration—namely, taking steps to make sure that a "celebrity pastor" culture does not develop around the senior leader. To keep a cult of personality from developing, several steps can be taken to limit the power of a senior pastor:

- Since most senior pastors are also the chair or moderator of the elder board, they have the ability to set agendas, control the flow of information, and dictate the overall direction of the elder board.[3] But there is no biblical requirement to have this structure. Indeed, it might be wise to have another elder in this slot so the senior pastor can't control the agenda and so there is a tangible expression of the senior pastor submitting himself to other leaders.

- Much of a pastor's standing and influence is because they do almost all the teaching and preaching in a church. Rotating the preaching schedule more regularly and allowing others to have visible time up front can keep the church from becoming overly focused on a single individual (though I recognize that in smaller churches this may be difficult).

- Giving a senior pastor the sole authority to hire and fire staff is a dangerous level of power and, as we have seen, creates a fear among staff members that he might use that power for retaliation. As an alternative, all hiring and firing recommendations could go first through an independent committee, composed of both elders and non-elders, including both men and women. For the purposes of our discussion, we'll call this the accountability committee (which could also have other functions we'll discuss). The committee would evaluate each staffing situation and then make recommendations to the elder board, which would make the final decision.

REAL FEEDBACK. If elder boards are to have an accurate portrayal of their own pastor's performance and character, then they need to have a careful annual review process by which feedback is communicated and relayed to the overall leadership body without the potential of reprisal upon those bringing the feedback. Here are a few ways this can be done:

- The annual review process needs to include not only the pastor's fellow elders (who are often his closest friends) but also those who work under the senior pastor, as well as several church members, including both men and women. Even though the church leadership would know who wrote these reviews, careful consideration should be given to whether the identity of the reviewers is revealed to the senior pastor. The senior pastor should certainly see the reviews, but it may be wise to keep at least some reviews anonymous so people can be frank and open without fear of retaliation.

- These annual reviews should *be shared openly with the entire elder board every year.* One of the reoccurring problems in most abuse cases is that the larger leadership body had no awareness of the ongoing issues with the senior pastor. When the problems eventually came out, they were shocked (and therefore more likely to believe that the victims were lying). The open dissemination of these reviews should help avoid that problem.

- Moreover, senior pastors should be required to do a careful and thorough annual review of each staff member under them. This practice is designed primarily to protect the staff from future retaliatory accusations from an abusive senior pastor. In one case of spiritual abuse, the senior pastor had not done written reviews of the staff for years and therefore was able to tell whatever stories he wanted about the employees' past behavior. If there had been a record of written reviews, the staff members would have had a way to defend themselves.

INDEPENDENT LEADERSHIP. As noted, an abusive leader often flourishes in situations where the people who hold him accountable are either his close friends or yes-men who are unable to stand up to him. If anyone does stand up to him, they are usually isolated and driven out. To address this concern, churches need to make sure that some of the leaders surrounding the senior pastor are genuinely independent of him. Here are a few suggestions:

- In the political world, *term limits* are often suggested as a way to root out career politicians who are loyal to the lobbyists and replace them with fresh, independent voices. For similar reasons, some churches have adopted a system where members of the elder board serve certain set terms and then roll off for a period of time.[4] That can be a healthy way to make sure the board continues to have new voices. Again, this may not be possible in small churches with a limited number of people who can serve as elders.

- Special attention should be given to the process by which new elders are added to the board so they aren't just the handpicked preferences of the senior pastor. It should be the congregation, not the pastor, that picks the elders. On this score, churches should be especially careful about allowing family members of the senior pastor to be on the board.

- In our discussion in chapter 4, Malcolm Gladwell observed that most organizations lack a "truth-teller" who comes from the outside, is not subject to the standard social hierarchies, and is willing to question what most take for granted. Admittedly, it can be hard to know how to get such individuals on an elder board or governing body. But I think churches can begin by acknowledging that they often pick elders who already fit within the traditional structures and paradigms. Put bluntly, some churches treat the elder board like the cool kid's club, where only certain people are invited. Rather, if elder boards sought out leaders who did not fit these existing paradigms, they might find more truth-tellers than they expected. This could include those from different social classes, different vocations, different educational backgrounds, or different ethnic and racial groups.

- One way to add independent, outside voices to the leadership structure is to invite women to participate. As already noted, women typically have very different perspectives on the church than the men, and their voices aren't always heard. For complementarian churches that have male-only elder boards, there are still ways this can be done. Recently, the Presbyterian Church in America (PCA) recommended to include women on official committees, and some churches are using women as nonvoting advisors on formal church commissions.[5] Whichever way it is done, women's voices can prevent the church leadership from becoming overly insular and ingrown.

One way that some churches have squelched this spirit of independent voices on the elder board is by insisting on a policy where *every decision of the elder board must be unanimous.* Such a policy says that the elder board can take a certain action only if there is 100 percent agreement. At first glance, this might seem like a healthy policy that promotes unity and harmony. Unfortunately, the opposite is the case. It protects abusive leaders from accountability and squashes dissenting opinion.[6]

When such a policy is enacted, members of the board feel less willing to speak their minds and less willing to be the lone "no" vote because they know it will derail the entire decision. Consequently, outlying voices on the elder board—voices that would normally offer healthy dissent—are pressured into going along with the rest of the board to maintain a unanimous vote. This creates an illusion of unity that isn't really there. And that illusion is promulgated even further when decisions of the elder board are represented to the congregation as "unanimous"—a representation that, at best, is misleading.

Moreover, abusive pastors use the requirement for unanimity to maintain power. Whenever an abusive leader wants to block something, all he needs is a single "no" vote from one of his loyal followers. Even worse, if his abuse comes to light, the elder board is unable to remove him because it requires a unanimous vote—something highly unlikely even in the best scenarios, especially if a pastor has loyal followers on the board. Theoretically, even if the entire board votes against him, the pastor can still vote "no" himself, which still prevents the vote from being unanimous!

GENUINE TRANSPARENCY. Spiritual abuse grows and thrives in church cultures that emphasize silence, secrecy, and self-protection. In contrast, churches that operate with openness and transparency build a culture that resists abuse. Here are a few ways to be more transparent:

- It might surprise you that in many denominations, the elders meeting is public and open to any church member. They are free to come and observe. Some churches even allow for questions. In certain circumstances that require confidentiality, an elder meeting might need to go to "executive session." But in most cases, church business is open business. It would be wise for churches to advertise the openness of their elder meetings and even encourage members to come. Holding the elders meeting in a larger venue like the church sanctuary or chapel is one way to encourage more people to attend. Churches might be surprised how differently their elders operate (in a good way) once other people are in the room watching them.
- Similarly, the minutes of the elders meetings should be made available to all church members, perhaps by posting on the church website. Again, this would exclude portions where the meeting was in executive session, but this provides some transparency about what is being discussed at these meetings and what decisions are being made.
- A key step toward transparency is for churches to develop a culture where people can freely raise questions or concerns

about the ministry of the church without being censored or silenced. Spiritually abusive churches are notorious for implementing no-talk rules (whether explicitly or implicitly), where staff or members aren't allowed to discuss the problems of the church with other people, ostensibly to avoid gossip or to keep factions from forming.[7] But this censorship is usually used to protect the power of the current leadership. As Johnson and VanVonderen observed, "Silence becomes the fortress wall of protection shielding the pastor's power position from scrutiny or challenge."[8] Here's one concrete suggestion: the church could have an annual public forum with opportunities for open exchanges about the state of the church, with a receptive rather than a defensive posture.

PROTECTION: CARING FOR THOSE WHO BRAVELY CALL OUT ABUSE

Even with a good prevention plan and accountability structure, there will still be instances of spiritual abuse in the church. When that happens, it is imperative that churches have a clear plan for how to handle those concerns when they are brought forward. Again, I recognize that each denomination has its own judicial process. The purpose here is not to create a new process or supersede those preexisting structures. Yet I offer the following suggestions, which can hopefully supplement that process and make it more effective in protecting those who are abused.

ABUSE TRAINING. Churches invest a lot of time into training their leaders—elders, deacons, and staff positions—about both theological and practical issues. And in recent years, many churches have emphasized training staff about child sexual abuse and how to spot it. Similarly, I think church staffs need to undertake some formal training in spiritual abuse. At a minimum, the elders need this sort of training, but arguably other key church leaders need it too. Pastors could even do a sermon series on God's vision for what authority and leadership in a church should look like and how it can be misconstrued. Openly discussing this issue can transform a church's culture because it reminds people of what Christian leadership ought to be.

AN ACCOUNTABILITY COMMITTEE. As noted, churches ought to consider having an accountability committee composed of elders and non-elders, including men and women. The purpose of this committee is to be a dedicated space to handle issues related to the senior pastor's job performance, as well as fielding any and all complaints related to the senior pastor's behavior (the committee should also deal with other high-level staff, given that abuse doesn't happen only in senior pastor roles). This committee would be the hub of the wheel when it comes to dealing with claims of spiritual abuse.

Part of the purpose of the accountability committee is protecting those who come forward with complaints. Bully pastors are able to retain control largely because they are able to retaliate against those who criticize them. The committee should be empowered to keep the victims safe from the abusive pastor. On this score, churches must be careful that the members of this committee are independently chosen and not merely the preferences of the senior pastor.

The committee should be required to provide full disclosure of its dealings to both the senior pastor and the elder board periodically so that it doesn't become a place to hide problems from the larger leadership body.

A POSTURE OF OPENNESS. As our modern culture has grown more aware of the problem of abuse, we hear a common mantra: "Believe the victims." If that implies that the victims' claims should automatically be accepted as proven, then it should be rejected. People should be considered innocent until proven guilty. But most don't use the mantra to mean that. Instead, it is often intended to communicate that organizations, including churches, should have a posture toward the accuser that is marked by sympathy and openness rather than suspicion and doubt. It's a shorthand way to say that churches should not assume the accuser is lying but to take their claims seriously. Or, put bluntly, the accuser should not be accused. They should be afforded the same rights as everyone else: *they* should be considered innocent until proven guilty.

Doesn't it seem that all churches would treat abuse claims with sympathy and openness? Unfortunately, that is not always the case. Time and again, people who step forward with concerns about an abusive leader's behavior are routinely viewed with suspicion, often discovering that they are the ones on trial. Instead of being shown sympathy, they are met with doubt and skepticism (often under the auspices of passages like Proverbs 18:17).

Imagine a scenario where a woman claims the senior pastor is harsh and heavy-handed. After she makes these claims, she soon finds herself in a room alone with a group of men who all happen to be close friends of the senior pastor. Suddenly they're peppering her with questions, essentially cross-examining her. It's not hard to imagine how she might feel like *she's* the one under investigation. And the scenario only gets worse when that senior pastor talks to these men offline, weaving a narrative about the woman, claiming she's difficult or hard to manage or insubordinate.

It is for these reasons that churches need to foster a culture of openness for those who come forward with claims of abuse. Again, no one is suggesting we do away with the presumption of innocence. Rather, we need to do away with the utterly prejudicial (not to mention unbiblical) default assumption that the accuser is lying. And that cultural shift begins with the accountability committee. At a minimum, that committee should be composed of those who embody an ethos of care, compassion, and sympathy.

THIRD-PARTY INVESTIGATION. Recent studies on spiritual abuse have highlighted multiple problems with the current system, but one of the most significant is the way abuse allegations are "investigated." Typically, such investigations are done in-house, often by friends or colleagues of the abusive pastor and by people who have no real training on how to identify abuse. Of course, many of these in-house investigations end up vindicating the abusive pastor. Again, this is precisely what happened with Bill Hybels, Steve Timmis, and James MacDonald. The initial "investigation" in each of these cases supposedly exonerated these leaders. It was only later, upon closer scrutiny, that the abuse was recognized.

These cases remind us that elder boards, church councils, and presbyteries can be in error. Not every decision they make is accurate or godly. And unless we are prepared to argue for the infallibility of the church, we have to acknowledge this possibility. As the Westminster Confession of Faith says, "All synods and councils, since the apostles' times, whether general or particular, may err; and many have erred."[9]

For example, consider the case of an Indiana pastor from the PCA.[10] Although this was a case of sexual abuse and not spiritual abuse, the same problems were evident. After five people came forward in 2019 with complaints about the pastor's inappropriate sexual behavior, the initial investigation of the presbytery concluded that there was "no presumption of guilt." But victims complained that the presbytery "mishandled" the case and "protected" the abusive pastor.[11] One of the victims complained, "They [the presbytery] were sometimes very dismissive towards us, very not trauma informed, very clearly favoring their colleagues throughout the whole thing."[12] One of the female, non-voting members of the investigative committee also noticed the bias. She argued that the commission interrogated the victims more vigorously than the pastor and even joked about how easily people think something is "sexual harassment."[13] Thankfully, a higher church court reviewed the case and decided there was sufficient evidence to put the pastor on trial after all.[14]

When a church is faced with credible claims of spiritual abuse, the standard practice should be to hire an independent, outside organization that understands how to investigate abuse cases properly (though I realize financial constraints may prevent some churches from doing so). Utilizing outside help does not negate or supersede the proper role of an elder board or presbytery; rather, it simply acknowledges that sometimes churches need expertise they may not be able to provide. The judicial process of a church and the use of an outside organization are not mutually exclusive. One more note: just because a church or organization *claims* the investigation is independent doesn't make it so. If the church remains in control of the process and in which findings are released, then it is not genuinely independent.[15]

PROCEDURAL-LEGAL GUIDANCE FOR THE VICTIMS. For those who've studied the judicial side of spiritual abuse cases, it is evident that the perpetrators often understand the legal-judicial-procedural rules of their denominations better than the victims. No doubt this is largely because the perpetrators are typically pastors who have a basic understanding of how the church courts operate, whereas the average victim is not a pastor and has no understanding of church courts, how to file a complaint, or what a trial might entail. In several cases I studied, the victims stumbled around in the dark about how to proceed, while the bully pastor quickly and efficiently lined up well-orchestrated legal roadblocks at every turn (often aided by sympathetic elders willing to fight for his cause). Again, the bully pastor gets all the support, and the victims get little.

To remedy this problem, I suggest churches make procedural-legal advice readily available to anyone who comes to the accountability committee with a complaint or concern. By "legal advice" I don't mean an attorney who operates in the American court systems (though one may be needed in some cases). Rather, I am referring to an expert in the judicial processes of that particular church or denomination who is not, in any way, relationally obligated to the church or its leadership. This latter point is key. This legal counsel needs to be a genuine third-party individual who will operate legitimately and fully for the victim.

VICTIM-SENSITIVE COMMUNICATION. From the testimonies I have read about abuse situations across the country, one reality quickly became evident: churches often don't communicate with the victims about the investigative process but do communicate with the abusive leader. Because the senior pastor is already "in the know" with his fellow elders or presbyters, he is often informed about developments and even given back-channel information. Meanwhile, the victims are often told nothing, often under the auspices of "confidentiality."

In contrast, churches and third-party investigative groups need to develop a victim-sensitive method of communication where the victims are involved from the start, given full disclosure about the progress of the investigation, and allowed to give input and feedback about the content of any public statements or reports.

COUNSELING AND SPIRITUAL CARE. As observed in chapter 6, the effects of spiritual abuse on the victims can be devastating. And the damage is not caused merely by the initial behavior of the abusive leader but by the long and excruciating process that unfolds after the victims come forward. For months, even years, the victims are subjected to the retaliatory tactics of abusive leaders: attacks on their character, broken relationships, legal wranglings, countercharges of slander, and more.

Sadly, most churches spend more time caring for the abusive pastor than for the victims. In case after case of abuse, most elder boards or presbyteries spent considerable time meeting with, counseling, and shepherding the abusive pastor and were minimally involved in caring for the victims.

Churches instead need to be proactive in supporting the victims spiritually, helping them walk through such an ordeal. Most helpful would be a third-party Christian counselor—preferably experienced in abuse cases—who could provide spiritual guidance and comfort to those who are hurting. Some churches may resist such a move, thinking that counsel from other pastors or elders on the church staff are all the victims need. But there are concerns with that approach. For one, these other pastors or elders are likely friends with the accused, making the victims wonder about their loyalties and whether they can be trusted. This doesn't mean the elders should be removed from the process or prevented from caring for the victims. It simply means churches should recognize that a third-party Christian counselor is an important step in the shepherding process.

SUMMARY. The care of those who call out abuse has a lot of moving pieces, so let me try to summarize by walking through a hypothetical example. Imagine a female church staff member is the director of a church's mercy ministry and works with and reports to the senior pastor. After years of domineering, heavy-handed treatment from the senior pastor, the woman finally decides to report the behavior. She goes to the accountability committee to share her story. That committee is composed of men and women who are trained (at least broadly) in how to spot abusive behavior and who exhibit a posture of sympathy and openness to such claims. Upon receiving the complaint, they might enact the following steps:

- Inform the elder board and the senior pastor that a complaint has been brought against the senior pastor and that they are exploring it further.
- Reassure the woman that the church loves her, that her concerns will be taken seriously, and that she will be protected from reprisal.
- Utilize a third-party Christian counselor, preferably trained

in abuse cases, to help walk the woman through any spiritual healing and recovery she might need.

- Offer procedural and legal guidance to the woman by using an outside, independent church counsel to inform the woman of her options in the church courts—for example, how church judicial proceedings work, how to file charges, and what a trial would entail.
- In consultation with the victim(s), hire an external third-party organization to thoroughly investigate the abuse claims.
- Make final recommendations to the board of elders who ultimately decide what should be done. In some churches, there may be higher governing bodies (for example, presbyteries, bishops) to which the board of elders can appeal for further help and guidance.

Keep in mind that this process is merely a recommendation; it may not fit exactly with the governing structure of any particular denomination. There are no doubt other ways that victims might be protected and abusive leaders held accountable. And no system is perfect. Even if the suggested steps are followed, the elder board may still refuse to hold the abusive leader accountable, despite the accountability committee's recommendations. But—and this is the key point—churches at least need to have a *plan* for how to handle abuse claims when they come. And the suggested process is one such plan.

CONCLUSION

All the prior chapters have led to this one. If spiritual abuse is a real problem in the church today (and it is), if this abuse is contrary to Scripture and disqualifying for ministry (and it is), if abusive leaders and churches often retaliate against the victims with cruel and aggressive tactics (and they do), and if these tactics are devastating to the lives of the victims (and they are), then there is only one conclusion: churches must *do something* to protect their sheep.

It's not enough to be aware. It's not enough to care. Churches must act. And this chapter has laid out three critical categories in which churches can take action. *Prevention*: Churches must do their best to weed out abusive candidates from the start by creating a vision for ministry that is radically biblical and therefore unattractive to leaders with abusive tendencies. *Accountability*: Too many churches have a culture of secrecy, self-protection, and image management—factors that create an ideal environment for spiritual abuse. In contrast, churches must create a culture that is open, transparent, and provides genuine accountability for its senior leadership. And finally, *Protection*: Churches must have a clear, well-organized plan for how to handle abuse claims and care for and protect the victims during the process.

A FINAL WORD TO CHRISTIAN LEADERS

The fear of loss is a path to the dark side.
—YODA

By now I hope it is clear what I have tried to accomplish in this book. I have written a book for Christian leaders about (of all things) bad Christian leaders—that is, pastors who are abusive bullies that mistreat their sheep in contradiction to all that God has called them to be in Scripture. We have tolerated this behavior for far too long, and we have an enormous debris field of broken lives and shattered churches to prove it. My goal has been to show that the problem of spiritual abuse is real, to give the proper definitions and diagnostic tools to identify it, and to motivate churches and Christian leaders to take the necessary steps to stop it.

But there is one final thing I want to do. I pray that this book will be helpful not only in stopping abusive leaders but also in preventing people from *becoming* abusive leaders. Most pastors don't start their ministries planning to be domineering and heavy-handed tyrants. Sometimes they find themselves, over time, morphing and changing into such a person, and they may not even realize it is happening. These changes are usually driven by the wear and tear of ministry, along with faulty philosophical commitments they may not even know they have.

That's where you, the reader, come in. You may be some sort of leader in the church. Maybe you're a pastor or an elder. If not, you are probably still deeply involved in ministry. And, no doubt, you have some influence at your church or Christian organization. In this epilogue I want to challenge some of the philosophical commitments that may be in your head, which, if left unchecked, may lead you down a worrisome path.

BEWARE MY-CHURCH-IS-THE-GREATEST SYNDROME

Okay, let's just get it out there. Most pastors believe *their* church is different. It has fixed all those pesky weaknesses found in *other* churches. Your church is not ingrown; it plants other churches. It's not doctrinally loose, but it's a church (finally!) that's theologically sound. It's not behind the times and out of date but in touch with culture and community. Or the opposite: it's not beholden to the culture but faithful to the past. It doesn't preach *that* way; it preaches *this* way. And on it goes. In short, we tend to think that no one does church quite like we do.

Now, that may sound a little blunt (and probably even a bit unfair). You might insist that you don't think that way. You have a sober, level-headed, realistic view of your ministry. Perhaps that's true. And if it is, that would be encouraging.

But after nearly thirty years of ministry—and many of those years spent training other ministers—I can tell you that genuinely humble assessments of one's own ministry are rare. Most pastors are tempted to believe (even if they wouldn't say it this way) that there is something unique and special and unprecedented about what they've done.

Don't misunderstand. I am not suggesting all churches are the same. Some are healthier than others. And God works through some churches in special ways, whereas others can be dead and lifeless. But the my-church-is-the-greatest syndrome can be a pathway to abuse if one's not careful. The prideful pastor begins to think he really is different from other people. Maybe he doesn't have to follow the rules others have to follow. And if anyone questions or challenges him, then he feels particularly free—indeed, he feels *obligated*—to squash such insubordination. How dare they criticize someone God has obviously blessed.

Pastors who believe their ministry is an indispensable, irreplaceable beacon on a hill also tend to be defensive if someone threatens to derail it or slow it down. "I can't let such naysayers stop an obvious work of the Holy Spirit," they might think. Therefore, they tell themselves that they must swiftly squelch such opposition—for the glory of God, of course.

So if you're a Christian leader teetering on the edge of my-church-is-the-greatest syndrome, then take a deep breath. God's church has been around for thousands of years, and it will be just fine. And Christianity will be just fine too if for some providential reason your church stays at only fifty people instead of growing to five hundred, or if it goes from five hundred and shrinks to fifty.

NO, THE SLIGHTEST DISAGREEMENT OR COMPLAINT WON'T SINK YOUR CHURCH

One thing I learned in my research for this book, and which I sort of already knew, is that pastors can be a worrisome bunch. They fret over many things, including budgets, attendance, and the overall vision of the church. But there is one worry that seems to haunt certain pastors: that *someone out there will speak negatively of them, which will in turn lead to division and sink the entire ministry.*

Certainly, the problem of grumbling and complaining in a congregation is not to be taken lightly. And left unchecked, it could swell into some sort of *coup d'état* where the church is split and the leadership is overthrown. But some pastors tend to catastrophize the slightest bit of disagreement or complaint in the church, thinking that even the smallest amount of dissension in the ranks will lead to a revolt. Some pastors are so worried about what is being said about them that it can lead to narcissistic paranoia.[1]

How is this attitude relevant to abuse? Because these pastors feel the need to squash the so-called rebellion before it gets out of the gate. They tend to overplay the danger, stoking fear around "slander" and "gossip," clamping down on anyone who seems to step out of line. They create a culture of silence where the church leadership can never be questioned or challenged (all under the auspices of protecting the peace and purity of the church).

But this supposed attempt to protect the peace and purity of the church can sometimes turn the church into a Gestapo-style entity, where people are watched, tracked, and monitored for any wayward statement. And if someone is caught breaking the rules, they're often prosecuted and brought up on charges. Needless to say, that doesn't feel like peace at all. Ironically, then, it may not be criticism from the congregation that sinks the church, but rather the overly defensive and heavy-handed tactics used to rebut the criticism.

So if you are a leader who bristles at criticism and sees all pushback as a reason to go to DEFCON 1, then you may need to rethink whether you have the disposition to be in the ministry. Church life is filled with complaints and criticisms—there's just no way around it.

Otherwise, it may be worth fostering a church culture where questions are allowed, criticisms are permitted, and people can freely and openly offer their pushback without retaliation. If you can receive such input humbly, with a thank you and a smile (even if the input is off the mark), you might discover that this openness is what builds the peace and purity of the church.

And who knows, some of the criticism may actually be right.

YOU AND THE ELDERS NEED MORE HELP THAN YOU THINK

Talking about congregations offering criticism and disagreement leads us to another problematic philosophical commitment that, left unchecked, can lead someone down the path of the bully pastor: the idea that the church's upper-level leadership—mainly the senior pastor but also the elders—does not need any help or input from members of the congregation to do its job.

After all, it is argued, the pastor and the elders are God's appointed leaders, given the rightful power and authority to rule the church. Thus, they must be utterly sufficient, in and of themselves, to make any decision or solve any problem. These leaders don't need advice or help from those they rule.

This attitude not only reflects a remarkable level of arrogance—which is concerning in its own right—but also displays a vividly *hierarchical* vision for the way the church should function. Essentially, it's *We are the boss; you are the servant. We are the rulers; you are the ruled. We tell you what to do; you don't presume to tell us what to do.*

Completely forgotten is how Jesus rebuked this hierarchical vision for leadership: "The rulers of the Gentiles lord it over them. . . . But it shall not be so among you. But whoever would be great among you must be your servant, and whoever would be first among you must be slave of all" (Mark 10:43–44).

Again, I am not denying the proper role of church leadership. And I am not suggesting there isn't authority in the church that requires church members to submit to their leaders (Heb. 13:17). But that authority can't be wielded in a way that is contrary to the image of leadership Christ has given us.

As an alternative, what if church leaders humbly recognized that they don't have all the answers? What if they acknowledged that they don't understand the perspective and situation of every church member or group or demographic and wanted to hear more? And what if they agreed that there is much to learn from the congregation about what the church should do and be?

If *that* were the attitude of the church's leadership, you would have a church culture that stands in direct opposition to abuse. You would have a culture that promotes peace and unity.

IF IT'S NEVER GOOD ENOUGH, THE PROBLEM MAY BE YOU

The church, while being the beautiful bride of Christ, is also a broken, inefficient, and clumsy organization. Sometimes the service doesn't start on time, maybe the deacons forget to get the air conditioning fixed before the summer heat kicked in, perhaps vacation Bible school does not have enough volunteers, and sometimes the sound team has the pulpit microphone all out of whack.

Any pastoral leader will want to address these sorts of issues on the staff team. Excellence is a biblical quality, and it is good and right to strive toward it. But for some church leaders, it seems like nothing is ever good enough. Staff teams crank out extra hours, volunteers exhaust themselves at the expense of their own families, and ministry leaders take on far too many commitments. And yet the pastor is never satisfied.

Consequently, an entire church culture can develop around "pleasing pastor Bob." The staff, and even church members, feel overloaded and heavily burdened, always walking on eggshells so that they don't have to endure more criticism from the pastor about how things weren't done well enough or quickly enough.

In this way, some church cultures can become remarkably legalistic. It's not that there is an explicit claim that people are saved by their good works (most pastors know better than that). But a works-oriented ethos develops around the senior leader—a meritocracy, if you will. A lot of law, very little grace, as everyone scrambles to make him happy. As Jesus said about the Pharisees, "They tie up heavy burdens, hard to bear, and lay them on people's shoulders" (Matt. 23:4).

Why do pastors behave this way? Sometimes it's because *when their church looks great, they look great.* And for abusive leaders, it's all about looking great. It's like parents who nitpick everything their child does, not out of love but because well-behaved children make them look good in front of others. Again, Jesus said the same thing of the Pharisees: "They do all their deeds to be seen by others" (Matt. 23:5). They liked the big stage. One might say the Pharisees were the first celebrity pastors.

As you read about the need to look great, you may be reminded of a pastor you know. Fair enough. But the question here is whether it describes *you*. Would your staff and your church members describe you this way? If so, your it's-never-good-enough approach, left unchecked, could be a pathway to becoming a bully pastor.

Again, Jesus's model of leadership is the opposite of abusive. He doesn't lay heavy burdens on the backs of his people. On the contrary, he invites us to rest: "Come to me, all who labor and are heavy laden, and I will give you rest. . . . For my yoke is easy, and my burden is light" (Matt. 11:28, 30).

MOST PEOPLE NEED A PAT ON THE BACK, NOT A KICK IN THE PANTS

While some pastors have a knack for finding the best in people, others constantly find the *worst* in them. A pastor once told me that the core of his philosophy of ministry was *confronting people's sin.* I was stunned and saddened. Apparently, this pastor thought his number one job was to go around looking for people's sin and confronting them about it. To be sure, he had what sounded like a pious reason for this approach: God hates sin and wants us to turn away from it. Thus, he saw himself as doing people a favor. They should be thanking him for always pointing out their sins!

It is true that God hates sin and wants us to turn away from it. And it is also true that there are times when pastors must confront people's sins. But that's not the primary calling of a shepherd. The job of the shepherd is to care for the sheep, and this includes feeding them, protecting them, encouraging them, binding up their wounds, and, yes, correcting them when needed. But anyone who makes correction and discipline the main thing is on the pathway to being an abusive pastor.

This misguided approach to ministry has predictable results. For one thing, it creates a culture of fault-finding where the pastor and his enablers are on a quest to discover everybody's sin patterns. Rather than thinking the best of others—"Love . . . hopes all things" (1 Cor. 13:7)—the pastor has an attitude of suspicion and judgment. Church members under oppressive leadership feel watched, beaten down, and criticized. They live in fear of making a mistake or stepping out of line.

In addition, a ministry bent on fault-finding in others can, and often does, warp the character of the one doing the fault-finding. These pastors tend to be prideful and condescending—after all, their time is spent looking at other people's faults rather than their own. Moreover, it can lead a pastor toward heavy-handed leadership of the sheep. Once he "discovers" their sins, then he has to confront them about their sins. And then, depending how they take it, he has to discipline them over those sins. Before long, the entire church culture becomes one of accusation and condemnation.

Again, it's not that different from abusive parents. Imagine a father who thinks his number one job is not to provide, protect, encourage, teach, and love his child but to perpetually correct his child's shortcomings. The bulk of his attention is devoted to discovering everything wrong with his thirteen-year-old son, which could be a full-time job if he wanted to make it such. And then he has to figure out how to discipline his son once he discovers such things. Before you know it, that father has created an oppressive and fearful household environment.

There are certainly times when a pastor has to correct their flock. But chances are your flock needs a compassionate pat on the back much more than it needs a swift kick in the pants. People in the church are hurting and discouraged and need someone to walk alongside them. In Psalm 23, the consummate psalm on God as our Shepherd, the focus is overwhelmingly on provision, protection, and comfort. Instead of a ministry of fault-finding, which can lead to abuse, we ought to pursue a ministry of encouragement and care, looking for the best in others rather than the worst.

On this score, we should heed the advice of the puritan Thomas Watson, "[A] humble Christian studies his own infirmities, and another's excellencies."[2] Or, as Matt Smethurst said, "If you are going to peer at others, become an expert in the evidences of grace you spot in their lives."[3]

YOUR SELF-AWARENESS MAY NOT BE AS ACCURATE AS YOU THINK

In spiritual abuse cases, it is standard fare to question whether the victims are seeing the situation clearly. Perhaps they are just imagining problems that aren't really there. Maybe their radar for relational and interpersonal issues is just not properly calibrated. Perhaps they are just overly sensitive.

Yet similar questions are hardly ever asked about the abusive pastor. Rarely is that pastor's own self-awareness questioned. Few seem as eager to raise doubts about his own relational intelligence and whether it is properly dialed in. People are less inclined to question whether the pastor is seeing those relationships clearly.

But this lopsided approach is rather remarkable if you pause for a moment to consider it. Aren't all human beings—pastors included—fallen, fallible creatures that don't always see clearly? Is it not also true that human beings, generally speaking, don't always have accurate perceptions of themselves? On top of this, it seems that pastors aren't necessarily the most relationally perceptive bunch. They often don't realize how they come across, how people perceive them, and how impactful (for good or for ill) their words are. And if the pastor is a narcissist—convinced of his own greatness—this problem is only exacerbated.

So here are some questions for you. When someone comes to you and says your words or actions have hurt them deeply, how do you react? Is your default assumption that this person has clearly misunderstood you and misconstrued what happened? Or is there ever a moment when you humbly ask whether you just might be the problem, even if you don't currently see it that way? Is there ever a time when you ask with Jesus's disciples, "Is it I, Lord?" (Matt. 26:22).

Such self-reflection would be particularly fitting if you have a track record of broken relationships and wounded sheep. Is there a "debris field" of broken lives in your wake? Do you explain it all away by telling yourself you are just a martyr, persecuted for faithfully "speaking the truth"? Or perhaps you tell yourself that the relational debris field is normal because good leaders are always under attack and have to defend themselves. Or maybe you've chalked it all up to demonic activity—it's just Satan trying to derail your godly ministry. In sum, have you convinced yourself that all these conflicts are everyone else's fault, even though you are the common denominator? If you do the math, that is pretty unlikely.

It's amazing what people will believe—no matter how incredible—to convince themselves that they are the good guy.

I am reminded of the story of Eustace in C. S. Lewis's *The Voyage of the Dawn Treader*. After falling asleep on a dragon's hoard, Eustace wakes up as a dragon. He's a frightening monster and doesn't even know it. When he sees two thin columns of smoke going up before his eyes, he doesn't realize it's coming from his own dragon nostrils.

Once he learns that he is a dragon, it causes him to do a little self-reflection. Even though he had been blaming everyone else on the ship for all his problems, he begins to realize "the others had not really been fiends at all."[4] Moreover—and here's where Lewis delivers the punch line—Eustace "began to wonder if he himself had been such a nice person as he always supposed."[5] In other words, Eustace realized he hadn't just become a dragon, he had *always* been a dragon. He was not the good guy he thought he was.

Many abusive leaders are like Eustace. They think they are pretty nice people and that everyone else is the problem. They frighten and scare people but don't understand why. They are a dragon but don't even know it.

If you are in leadership, ask the Lord to give you the humility to admit you may not see yourself as you really are. Be willing to take a long, hard look at yourself to see if you, like Eustace, have columns of smoke coming up from your nostrils. If you do, turn to Aslan and ask him to do what only he can do: make you whole again.

CONCLUSION

This epilogue has been focused on you, the reader. My concern is not just that you stop bully pastors but also that you not become a bully pastor or leader yourself. Thus, I have taken a tour through some problematic philosophies and approaches that can define a ministry and shown how they can lead to abusive tendencies if one is not careful.

When you look at all the missteps mentioned, a common thread unites them: *fear.*

Pastors who think their church is the best fear losing it. Pastors who worry about any complaint or dissent fear division. Pastors institute a hierarchical leadership because they fear their authority being disrespected. Pastors are hard to please and unduly burden their staff because they fear looking bad. Pastors become oppressive fault-finders out of fear of having an ill-behaved congregation that reflects poorly on them. And, finally, pastors insist they are seeing themselves accurately and that everyone else is to blame because they are afraid of discovering they may not be the good guy they suppose.

What's the problem with all this fear? Yoda said it best: "The fear of loss is a path to the dark side."[6] It is tragic what people will do and who they will become to avoid loss—to avoid losing the church they've built. Indeed, if necessary, they will become heavy-handed tyrants to the very people they are supposed to love and protect.

Joel Brown, one of the pastors at Mars Hill Church, explains how this precise fear drove the abusive behavior of Mark Driscoll: "There always was this underlying assumption that Mark had that people were trying to take his power; people were trying to take his church from him. . . . There was this constant desire to protect his power and to make sure he maintained control."[7]

Such fear of loss is idolatrous. It puts something else—in this case, our own glory, power, and success—above the good of God's sheep and above the glory and honor of God himself.

Jesus knew this would be a problem. He knew that the biggest obstacle to a healthy ministry would be fear of loss, fear of suffering. So he tackled this problem head-on. His solution is the point of this whole book: "If anyone would come after me, let him deny himself and take up his cross and follow me. For whoever would save his life will lose it, but whoever loses his life for my sake and the gospel's will save it" (Mark 8:34–35).

The answer to the abusive pastor was there all the time. It is the cross of Christ. There, on display for all the world to see, was a shepherd who did not save his own life but gave it up freely for the sake of others.

And anyone called to the ministry must do the same.

NOTES

INTRODUCTION

1. Mike Cosper's excellent podcast published by Christianity Today, *The Rise and Fall of Mars Hill*, highlighted these cases in new and fresh ways. However, my concerns and the writing of this book began years before those episodes published.

2. See Wade Mullen, *Something's Not Right: Decoding the Hidden Tactics of Abuse and Freeing Yourself from Its Power* (Carol Stream, IL: Tyndale, 2020); Lisa Oakley and Kathryn Kinmond, *Breaking the Silence on Spiritual Abuse* (New York: Palgrave Macmillan, 2013), 89–119. A very helpful article on abuse, forgiveness, and substitutionary atonement is Jacob and Rachael Denhollander, "Justice: The Foundation of a Christian Approach to Abuse," *Fathom*, November 19, 2018, https://www.fathommag.com/stories/justice-the-foundation-of-a-christian-approach-to-abuse.

3. Jamiles Larty and Abbie VanSickle, "'Don't Kill Me': Others Tell of Abuse by Officer Who Knelt on George Floyd," *New York Times*, February 2, 2021, https://www.nytimes.com/2021/02/02/us/derek-chauvin-george-floyd-past-cases.html.

CHAPTER 1: THE FIRST SHALL BE FIRST

1. Sam Allberry, "How Do Churches End Up with Domineering Bullies for Pastors?," *The Gospel Coalition*, January 21, 2019, https://www.thegospelcoalition.org/article/domineering-bullies-pastors/.

2. Collin Hansen, "Editor's Choice: The Best of 2019," *The Gospel Coalition*, December 16, 2019, https://www.thegospelcoalition.org/article/editors-choice-the-best-of-2019/.

3. Sarah Pulliam Bailey, "Mark Driscoll Charged with Abusive Behavior by 21 Former Mars Hill Pastors," *Religion News Service*, August 22, 2014, https://religionnews.com/2014/08/22/mark-driscoll -charged-allegations-21-former-mars-hill-pastors/. After I had begun writing this book, a more updated assessment of Mars Hill and Driscoll's leadership was released by Mike Cosper, *The Rise and Fall of Mars Hill*, podcast for *Christianity Today*, https://www .christianitytoday.com/ct/podcasts/rise-and-fall-of-mars-hill/.

4. Janet I. Tu, "Mars Hill Church Reeling as Pastor Mark Driscoll Quits," *Seattle Times*, October 16, 2014, https://www.seattletimes.com /seattle-news/mars-hill-church-reeling-as-pastor-mark-driscoll-quits/.

5. Brandon Ambrosino, "Megachurch Pastor Mark Driscoll Was an Evangelical Rock Star. Here's How He Fell from Grace," *Vox*, August 24, 2014, https://www.vox.com/2014/8/24/6050155/mega church-pastor-mark-driscoll-was-an-evangelical-rock-star-heres.

6. Julie Roys, "Hard Times at Harvest," *World*, December 13, 2018, https://world.wng.org/2018/12/hard_times_at_harvest.

7. https://www.julieroys.com/wp-content/uploads/2018/10/THE-Letter -to-HBC-Elders-2013.pdf.

8. Roys, "Hard Times at Harvest."

9. Roys, "Hard Times at Harvest."

10. Roys, "Hard Times at Harvest."

11. Kate Shellnutt, "Harvest Elders Say James MacDonald Is 'Biblically Disqualified' from Ministry," *Christianity Today*, November 5, 2019, https://www.christianitytoday.com/news/2019/november/harvest -elders-say-james-macdonald-biblically-disqualified.html.

12. Will E. Young, "Inside Liberty University's 'Culture of Fear,'" *Washington Post*, July 24, 2019, https://www.washingtonpost.com/out look/2019/07/24/inside-liberty-universitys-culture-fear-how-jerry -falwell-jr-silences-students-professors-who-reject-his-pro-trump -politics/?arc404=true.

13. Carol Kuruvilla, "Why a Sex Scandal Toppled Jerry Falwell Jr. When It Seemed Like Nothing Else Could," *Huffington Post*, August 26, 2020, https://www.huffpost.com/entry/jerry-falwell-sex -liberty_n_5f4420d4c5b66a80ee16897c.

14. Daniel Silliman, "The Christian Peacemaker Who Left a Trail of Trauma," *Christianity Today*, November 16, 2021, https://www

.christianitytoday.com/news/2021/november/judy-dabler-creative
-conciliation-abuse-lapm-unfit-ministry.html.

15. Heather Tomlinson, "Spiritual Abuse," *Premier Christianity*, February 4, 2014, https://www.premierchristianity.com/home/spiritual
-abuse/3613.article.

16. Lisa Oakley and Justin Humphreys, *Understanding Spiritual Abuse in Christian Communities* (Bournemouth, UK: The National Centre for Post-Qualifying Social Work and Professional Practice, 2018), 3.

17. Limitations with the methodology were explored by the Evangelical Alliance Theology Advisory Group, *Reviewing the Discourse of "Spiritual Abuse": Logical Problems and Unintended Consequences* (Evangelical Alliance, 2018).

18. Some of these key resources include Wade Mullen, *Something's Not Right: Decoding the Hidden Tactics of Abuse and Freeing Yourself from Its Power* (Carol Stream, IL: Tyndale, 2020); Lisa Oakley and Kathryn Kinmond, *Breaking the Silence on Spiritual Abuse* (New York: Palgrave Macmillan, 2013), 89–119; Lisa Oakley and Justin Humphreys, *Escaping the Maze of Spiritual Abuse: Creating Healthy Christian Cultures* (London: SPCK, 2019); Chuck DeGroat, *When Narcissism Comes to Church: Healing Your Community from Emotional and Spiritual Abuse* (Downers Grove, IL: InterVarsity Press, 2020); Scot McKnight and Laura Barringer, *A Church Called Tov: Forming a Goodness Culture That Resists Abuses of Power and Promotes Healing* (Carol Stream, IL: Tyndale, 2020); David Johnson and Jeff VanVonderen, *The Subtle Power of Spiritual Abuse: Recognizing and Escaping Spiritual Manipulation and False Spiritual Authority within the Church* (Minneapolis: Bethany House, 1991); and Ken Blue, *Healing Spiritual Abuse: How to Break Free from Bad Church Experiences* (Downers Grove, IL: InterVarsity Press, 1993).

19. Kate Shellnutt, "Acts 29 CEO Removed Amid 'Accusations of Abusive Leadership,'" *Christianity Today*, February 7, 2020, https://www.christianitytoday.com/news/2020/february/acts-29-ceo-steve-timmis
-removed-spiritual-abuse-tch.html. For a more detailed report on the Timmis case, see *An Independent Learning Review: The Crowded House* (Thirtyone:eight, 2020), https://thirtyoneeight.org/media/2678
/the-crowded-house-learning-review-full-report.pdf.

20. Shellnutt, "Acts 29 CEO Removed."

21. Shellnutt, "Acts 29 CEO Removed."
22. Shellnutt, "Acts 29 CEO Removed."
23. Shellnutt, "Acts 29 CEO Removed."
24. Shellnutt, "Acts 29 CEO Removed."
25. DeGroat, *When Narcissism Comes to Church*, 3, 143.
26. For an example, see Gregory Nazianzen and his treatise on bad priests in his day: Oration II, "In Defence of His Flight to Pontus, and His Return, after His Ordination to the Priesthood, with an Exposition of the Character of the Priestly Office," 78–85.
27. Jim Collins, *From Good to Great: Why Some Companies Make the Leap and Others Don't* (New York: HarperBusiness, 2001). In particular, note how Collins describes "Level 5" leaders are different than "celebrity leaders" (39-40).
28. John Chrysostom, *Six Books on the Priesthood*, trans. Graham Neville, Popular Patristics Series (Crestwood, NY: St Vladimir's Seminary Press, 2002), 3.9.
29. DeGroat, *When Narcissism Comes to Church*. See also Johannes Brunzel, "Overconfidence and Narcissism among the Upper Echelons: A Systematic Literature Review," *Management Review Quarterly* 71 (2021): 585–623, https://doi.org/10.1007/s11301-020-00194-6.
30. DeGroat, *When Narcissism Comes to Church*, 7.
31. McKnight and Barringer, *A Church Called Tov*, 184.
32. Paul David Tripp, *Lead: 12 Principles for Gospel Leadership in the Church* (Wheaton, IL: Crossway, 2020), 104.
33. Martin Bucer, *Concerning the True Care of Souls*, trans. Peter Beale (Carlisle, PA: The Banner of Truth Trust, 2009), 57.
34. Michael Jensen, "Recovering the Art of Gentleness," *ABC Religion and Ethics*, November 24, 2021, https://www.abc.net.au/religion/michael-jensen-art-of-gentleness/13647030.
35. Mullen, *Something's Not Right*, 33–52.
36. Brendan Kiley, "Why the Mars Hill Faithful Have Started to Question Mark," *Stranger*, July 30, 2014, https://www.thestranger.com/seattle/why-the-mars-hill-faithful-have-started-to-question-mark/Content?oid=20257920.
37. Kiley, "Why the Mars Hill Faithful Have Started to Question Mark."
38. Kiley, "Why the Mars Hill Faithful Have Started to Question Mark."

39. Numerous books have cataloged the collapse of trust in institutions, especially government, science, and higher education; for example, Christopher Hayes, *Twilight of the Elites: America after Meritocracy* (New York: Crown, 2012); Douglas E. Schoen, *The End of Authority: How Loss of Legitimacy and Broken Trust Are Endangering Our Future* (New York: Rowman and Littlefield, 2013); Tom Nichols, *The Death of Expertise: The Campaign against Established Knowledge and Why It Matters* (New York: Oxford, 2017).

40. Tripp, *Lead*, 134.

41. Brian Sanders, *Life after Church: God's Call to Disillusioned Christians* (Downers Grove, IL: InterVarsity Press, 2007); Julia Duin, *Quitting Church: Why the Faithful Are Fleeing and What to Do about It* (Grand Rapids: Baker, 2008); Dan Kimball, *They Like Jesus but Not the Church: Insights from Emerging Generations* (Grand Rapids: Zondervan, 2007); and David Kinnaman, *You Lost Me: Why Young Christians Are Leaving Church . . . And Rethinking Faith* (Grand Rapids: Baker, 2016).

42. For more on this theme, see John Dickson, *Bullies and Saints: An Honest Look at the Good and Evil of Christian History* (Grand Rapids: Zondervan, 2021).

43. Chrysostom, *Six Books on the Priesthood*, 3.15.

44. Dickson, *Bullies and Saints*, 275–82.

CHAPTER 2: THAT WHICH SHALL NOT BE NAMED

1. For a helpful treatment of domestic violence, see Darby Strickland, *Is It Abuse? A Biblical Guide to Identifying Domestic Abuse and Helping Victims* (Phillipsburg, NJ: P&R, 2020).

2. The Bill Hybels case is covered extensively in Scot McKnight and Laura Barringer, *A Church Called Tov: Forming a Goodness Culture That Resists Abuses of Power and Promotes Healing* (Carol Stream, IL: Tyndale, 2020).

3. For a helpful overview of emotional and psychological abuse (though I have significant disagreement on certain points), see Shannon Thomas, *Healing from Hidden Abuse: A Journey through Stages of Recovery from Psychological Abuse* (MAST Publishing House, 2016).

4. The Evangelical Alliance Theology Advisory Group, *Reviewing the Discourse of "Spiritual Abuse": Logical Problems and Unintended*

Consequences (Evangelical Alliance, 2018). For a similar sort of objection to the term *spiritual abuse*, see Krish Kandiah, "Does the Church's First Spiritual Abuse Verdict Give Critics a New Weapon?," *Christianity Today*, January 12, 2018, https://www.christianitytoday .com/ct/2018/january-web-only/spiritual-abuse-church-england-guilty -verdict-ccpas-survey.html.

5. Evangelical Alliance, *Reviewing the Discourse of "Spiritual Abuse,"* 3.
6. It should be acknowledged that spiritual abuse can also happen outside the church, for example, in a marriage. See Darby Strickland, "Spiritual Abuse in Marriage (Part 1)," *CCEF*, September 18, 2019, https://www.ccef.org/spiritual-abuse-in-marriage/.
7. James Bannerman, *The Church of Christ*, vol. 1 (Edinburgh: Banner of Truth, 1960), 247–48.
8. Again, see Strickland, "Spiritual Abuse in Marriage (Part 1)."
9. This definition is my own. For a helpful overview (and comparison) of different definitions, see Lisa Oakley and Kathryn Kinmond, *Breaking the Silence on Spiritual Abuse* (New York: Palgrave Macmillan, 2013), 20–22.
10. Of course, this doesn't mean all spiritual abuse happens downward. Oakley and Kinmond argue that there are other models of spiritual abuse (though not ones we are considering here) where abuse can happen by those in "parallel and lower positions" (*Breaking the Silence*, 16). See also, Lisa Oakley and Kathryn Kinmond, "Developing Safeguarding Policy and Practice for Spiritual Abuse," *Journal of Adult Protection* 16, no. 2 (April 2014): 91, https://doi.org/10.1108/JAP -07-2013-0033.
11. David Johnson and Jeff VanVonderen, *The Subtle Power of Spiritual Abuse: Recognizing and Escaping Spiritual Manipulation and False Spiritual Authority within the Church* (Minneapolis: Bethany House, 1991), 20, emphasis original.
12. Demaris S. Wehr, "Spiritual Abuse: When Good People Do Bad Things," in *The Psychology of Mature Spirituality: Integrity, Wisdom, Transcendence*, ed. Polly Young-Eisendrath and Melvin E. Miller (New York: Routledge, 2000), 47–61. I disagree with a number of aspects of Wehr's article, but there are also many common grace insights.
13. Bannerman, *Church of Christ*, 248. For a similar warning from

the seventeenth century, see Richard Baxter, *The Reformed Pastor* (Carlisle, PA: Banner of Truth, 1983), 144.

14. Matthew Henry, *Matthew Henry's Commentary* (New York: Revell, 1975), 6:1105.

15. Henry, *Commentary*, 5:291.

16. Lisa Oakley and Justin Humphreys, *Escaping the Maze of Spiritual Abuse: Creating Healthy Christian Cultures* (London: SPCK, 2019), 53–59.

17. Mike Cosper, "You Read the Bible, Ringo?," July 7, 2021, in *The Rise and Fall of Mars Hill*, produced by *Christianity Today*, podcast, quote at 42:40–44:57, https://www.christianitytoday.com/ct/podcasts/rise -and-fall-of-mars-hill/rise-fall-mars-hill-podcast-bible-ringo.html.

18. Cosper, "You Read the Bible, Ringo?," quote at 46:51–47:47.

19. For a deeper dive into some of these issues, see David J. Ward, "The Lived Experience of Spiritual Abuse," *Mental Health, Religion, and Culture* 14, no. 9 (2011): 899–915, https://doi.org/10.1080/13674676.20 10.536206.

20. Ward, "The Lived Experience of Spiritual Abuse," 909.

21. Oakley and Humphreys, *Escaping the Maze of Spiritual Abuse*, 46.

22. For more on the damage words can cause, see Jeff Robinson, *Taming the Tongue: How the Gospel Transforms Our Talk* (Austin, TX: The Gospel Coalition, 2021).

23. Valerie Tarico, "Christian Right Mega-Church Minister Faces Mega-Mutiny for Alleged Abusive Behavior," *Salon*, April 3, 2014, https://www.salon.com/2014/04/03/christian_right_mega_church _minister_faces_mega_muntiny_for_abusive_behavior_partner/.

24. "Former Harvest Bible Staffers Accuse James MacDonald of Lavish Vacations on the Church's Dime," *Relevant*, March 13, 2019, https://www.relevantmagazine.com/faith/church/former-harvest -bible-staffers-accuse-james-macdonald-of-lavish-vacations-on-the -churchs-dime/.

25. DeGroat, *When Narcissism Comes to Church*, 92. See also Oakley and Humphreys, *Escaping the Maze of Spiritual Abuse*, 51–52.

26. That letter can be found at the bottom of the following article: Julie Roys, "Acts 29 President Matt Chandler Under Fire for Removing Staff Alleging Abuse and Changing Story about Removal of CEO," *Roys Report*, February 13, 2020, https://julieroys.com/acts

-29-president-matt-chandler-under-fire-for-removing-staff-alleging
-abuse-changing-story-about-removal-of-ceo/.

27. Kenneth J. Garrett, *In the House of Friends: Understanding and Healing from Spiritual Abuse in Christian Churches* (Eugene, OR: Wipf and Stock, 2020), 48.

28. Ronan Farrow, "Harvey Weinstein's Army of Spies," *New Yorker*, November 6, 2017, https://www.newyorker.com/news/news-desk /harvey-weinsteins-army-of-spies.

29. DeGroat, *When Narcissism Comes to Church*, 91–92.

30. DeGroat, *When Narcissism Comes to Church*, 75.

31. Johnson and VanVonderen, *Subtle Power of Spiritual Abuse*, 63–64.

32. DeGroat, *When Narcissism Comes to Church*, 82; Wade Mullen, *Something's Not Right: Decoding the Hidden Tactics of Abuse and Freeing Yourself from Its Power* (Carol Stream, IL: Tyndale, 2020), 33–52.

33. Johnson and VanVonderen, *Subtle Power of Spiritual Abuse*, 23.

34. Ken Blue, *Healing Spiritual Abuse: How to Break Free from Bad Church Experiences* (Downers Grove, IL: InterVarsity Press, 1993), 12–13. See also Oakley and Humphreys, *Escaping the Maze of Spiritual Abuse*, 104–105.

35. Wehr, "Spiritual Abuse," 54.

36. Oakley and Humphreys, *Escaping the Maze of Spiritual Abuse*, 105.

37. For an example, Philip Gulley, *If the Church Were Christian: Rediscovering the Values of Jesus* (San Francisco: HarperOne, 2010), argues that believing in original sin engenders "spiritual abuse" (40; cf. 30).

38. Blue, *Healing Spiritual Abuse*, 13.

39. Oakley and Kinmond, *Breaking the Silence*, 66.

CHAPTER 3: A HEAVY YOKE ON US

1. Derek Kidner, *Genesis* (Downers Grove, IL: IVP Academic, 2008), 76.

2. G. K. Beale, *The Temple and the Church's Mission: A Biblical Theology of the Dwelling Place of God* (Downers Grove, IL: InterVarsity Press, 2004).

3. Beale, *The Temple and Church's Mission*, 66.

4. Ralph W. Klein, *1 Samuel*, Word Biblical Commentary (Waco, TX: Word, 1983), 78–79.

5. Bill T. Arnold, *1 & 2 Samuel*, NIV Application Commentary (Grand Rapids: Zondervan, 2003), 151–52.

6. Arnold, *1 & 2 Samuel*, 151.

7. August H. Konkel, *1 & 2 Kings*, NIV Application Commentary (Grand Rapids: Zondervan, 2006), 241.

8. Daniel I. Block, *The Book of Ezekiel: Chapters 25–48*, New International Commentary on the Old Testament (Grand Rapids: Eerdmans, 1998), 279–83.

9. Timothy S. Laniak, *Shepherds After My Own Heart: Pastoral Traditions and Leadership in the Bible* (Downers Grove, IL: InterVarsity Press, 2006), 151.

10. Block, *Book of Ezekiel*, 283–284.

11. Laniak, *Shepherds After My Own Heart*, 152.

12. Klein, *1 Samuel*, 25.

13. Josephus, *Ant.* 15–18.

14. R. T. France, *The Gospel of Mark* (Grand Rapids: Eerdmans, 2002), 415–16.

15. Robert H. Stein, *Mark*, Baker Exegetical Commentary on the New Testament (Grand Rapids: Baker Academic, 2008), 484.

16. France, *Mark*, 419.

17. John Calvin, *Commentary on a Harmony of the Evangelists, Matthew, Mark, and Luke, Vol. 1*, trans. William Pringle (Grand Rapids: Baker, 1993), 424 (emphasis original).

18. Johannes P. Louw and Eugene A. Nida, *Greek-English Lexicon of the New Testament: Based on Semantic Domains* (New York: United Bible Societies, 1989), 88.137 (p.757).

19. See discussion in William D. Mounce, *Pastoral Epistles*, Word Biblical Commentary (Nashville: Thomas Nelson, 2000), 176.

20. Johannes Brunzel, "Overconfidence and Narcissism among the Upper Echelons: A Systematic Literature Review," *Management Review Quarterly* 71 (2021): 585–623, https://doi.org/10.1007/s11301-020-00194-6.

21. Dane Ortlund, *Gentle and Lowly: The Heart of Christ for Sinners and Sufferers* (Wheaton, IL: Crossway, 2020), 19.

22. Ortlund, *Gentle and Lowly*, 19.

23. John Chrysostom, *Six Books on the Priesthood*, trans. Graham Neville,

Popular Patristics Series (Crestwood, NY: St Vladimir's Seminary Press, 2002), 3.7.

24. Julie Roys, "Hard Times at Harvest," *World*, December 13, 2018, https://world.wng.org/2018/12/hard_times_at_harvest.

25. Karen H. Jobes, *1 Peter*, Baker Exegetical Commentary on the New Testament (Grand Rapids: Baker Academic, 2005), 305.

26. Mounce, *Pastoral Epistles*, 535.

CHAPTER 4: A TRAIL OF DEAD BODIES

1. *Aliens*, directed by James Cameron (Brandywine Productions, 1986).

2. There is an ongoing discussion about whether "ravenous wolves" know they're "ravenous wolves." In other words, does an abusive pastor have to know he's being abusive to receive such a description? (see Lisa Oakley and Justin Humphreys, *Escaping the Maze of Spiritual Abuse: Creating Healthy Christian Cultures* [London: SPCK, 2019], 113–15). But I see no biblical reason why the term should be reserved only for those who are fully aware of what they are doing; often wolves are deceived about their own actions and identity. Of course, there's a continuum here. Some are more aware than others, which certainly increases their culpability.

3. Chuck DeGroat, *When Narcissism Comes to Church: Healing Your Community from Emotional and Spiritual Abuse* (Downers Grove, IL: InterVarsity Press, 2020), 3, 143.

4. DeGroat, *When Narcissism Comes to Church*, 91.

5. DeGroat, *When Narcissism Comes to Church*, 3, 143.

6. For a broader perspective on institutional betrayal, see Carly Parnitzke Smith and Jennifer Freyd, "Institutional Betrayal," *American Psychologist* 69, no. 6 (September 2014): 575–87, https://doi.org/10.1037/a0037564.

7. Lisa Oakley and Kathryn Kinmond, *Breaking the Silence on Spiritual Abuse* (New York: Palgrave Macmillan, 2013), 14.

8. Wade Mullen, *Something's Not Right: Decoding the Hidden Tactics of Abuse and Freeing Yourself from Its Power* (Carol Stream, IL: Tyndale, 2020), 18 (emphasis mine).

9. Kate Shellnutt, "Acts 29 CEO Removed Amid 'Accusations of Abusive Leadership,'" *Christianity Today*, February 7, 2020, https://www

.christianitytoday.com/news/2020/february/acts-29-ceo-steve-timmis
-removed-spiritual-abuse-tch.html.

10. Malcolm Gladwell, *Talking to Strangers: What We Should Know about
the People We Don't Know* (New York: Little, Brown, and Company,
2019), 73 (emphasis his).

11. Gladwell, *Talking to Strangers*, 130.

12. Oakley and Kinmond, *Breaking the Silence*, 61.

13. Gladwell, *Talking to Strangers*, 99.

14. Gladwell, *Talking to Strangers*, 99.

15. As cited in Gladwell, *Talking to Strangers*, 99.

16. Jennifer Michelle Greenberg, *Not Forsaken: A Story of Life after Abuse*
(London: The Good Book Company, 2019), 44.

17. Oakley and Humphreys, *Escaping the Maze of Spiritual Abuse*, 98–99.

18. Basyle Tchividjian and Justin S. Holcomb, *Caring for Survivors of
Sexual Abuse: Being Comfortable in Your Own Skin* (Greensboro, NC:
New Growth, 2017), 10.

19. Daniel Silliman, "The Christian Peacemaker Who Left a Trail
of Trauma," *Christianity Today*, November 16, 2021, https://www
.christianitytoday.com/news/2021/november/judy-dabler-creative
-conciliation-abuse-lapm-unfit-ministry.html.

20. Silliman, "Christian Peacemaker."

21. J. R. R. Tolkien, *The Two Towers* (New York: HarperCollins, 1999),
223.

22. Tolkien, *Two Towers*, 225.

23. Tolkien, *Two Towers*, 226.

24. Tolkien, *Two Towers*, 223.

25. Tolkien, *Two Towers*, 226.

26. Tolkien, *Two Towers*, 225.

27. Tolkien, *Two Towers*, 227.

28. Tolkien, *Two Towers*, 229.

CHAPTER 5: FLIPPING THE SCRIPT

1. Manya Brachear Pashman and Jeff Coen, "After Years of Inquiries,
Willow Creek Pastor Denies Misconduct Allegations," *Chicago
Tribune*, March 23, 2018, https://www.chicagotribune.com/news
/breaking/ct-met-willow-creek-pastor-20171220-story.html.

2. Pashman and Coen, "Willow Creek Pastor Denies Misconduct Allegations."

3. Laurie Goodstein, "He's a Superstar Pastor: She Worked for Him and Says He Groped Her Repeatedly," *New York Times*, August 5, 2018, https://www.nytimes.com/2018/08/05/us/bill-hybels-willow -creek-pat-baranowski.html.

4. Kate Shellnutt, "Willow Creek Investigation: Allegations against Bill Hybels Are Credible," *Christianity Today*, February 28, 2019, https://www.christianitytoday.com/news/2019/february/willow-creek -bill-hybels-investigation-iag-report.html.

5. Emily McFarlan Miller, "Misconduct Allegations against Willow Creek Founder Bill Hybels Are Credible, Independent Report Finds," *Washington Post*, March 1, 2019, https://www.washingtonpost .com/religion/2019/03/01/independent-report-finds-allegations -against-willow-creek-founder-bill-hybels-are-credible/.

6. Miller, "Misconduct Allegations."

7. Emily McFarlan Miller, "Willow Creek Elders and Lead Pastor Resign in Wake of Hybels Revelations," *Religion News Service*, August 8, 2018, https://religionnews.com/2018/08/08/willow-creek -elders-and-lead-pastor-resign-in-wake-of-hybels-revelations/.

8. F. Remy Diederich, *Broken Trust: A Practical Guide to Identify and Recover from Toxic Faith, Toxic Church, and Spiritual Abuse* (Columbia, SC: LifeChange, 2017), 75.

9. *Wag the Dog*, directed by Barry Levinson (Baltimore Pictures and TriBeCa Productions, 1997).

10. The ESV reads, "If your brother sins *against you*" (Matt 18:15). The italicized words are missing in some early Christian manuscripts, which is why some other English translations leave them out. But the preponderance of textual witnesses contains these words, including many of the church fathers, leading many scholars to favor the originality of the words; for example, W. D. Davies and D. C. Allison, *The Gospel According to Saint Matthew*, ICC (Edinburgh: T&T Clark, 1997), 782 n. 3; R. H. Gundry, *Matthew: A Commentary on His Handbook for a Mixed Church under Persecution* (Grand Rapids: Eerdmans, 1994), 367; David L. Turner, *Matthew*, Baker Exegetical Commentary on the New Testament (Grand Rapids: Baker Academic, 2008), 444.

11. Scot McKnight and Laura Barringer, *A Church Called Tov: Forming a Goodness Culture That Resists Abuses of Power and Promotes Healing* (Carol Stream, IL: Tyndale, 2020), 49. See also, Erwin W. Lutzer, *When You've Been Wronged: Moving from Bitterness to Forgiveness* (Chicago: Moody, 2007), 140.

12. Craig L. Blomberg, "On Building and Breaking Barriers: Forgiveness, Salvation and Christian Counseling with Special Reference to Matthew 18:15–35," *Journal of Psychology and Christianity* 25, no. 2 (2006): 138, https://ixtheo.de/Record/1644497689.

13. McKnight and Barringer, *Church Called Tov*, 49.

14. Morgan Lee, "Why Steve Timmis Was Accused of 'Spiritual Abuse,'" February 13, 2020, in *Quick to Listen*, produced by *Christianity Today*, podcast, quote at 33:50, https://www.christianity today.com/ct/podcasts/quick-to-listen/steve-timmis-crowded-house-spiritual-abuse-acts29.html.

15. Pashman and Coen, "Willow Creek Pastor Denies Misconduct Allegations."

16. Mike Cosper, "I Kissed Christianity Goodbye," August 19, 2021, in *The Rise and Fall of Mars Hill*, produced by *Christianity Today*, podcast, quote at 15:48, https://www.christianitytoday.com/ct /podcasts/rise-and-fall-of-mars-hill/.

17. Daniel Silliman, "RZIM Will No Longer Do Apologetics," *Christianity Today*, March 10, 2021, https://www.christianitytoday .com/news/2021/march/ravi-zacharias-rzim-name-change-abuse -victims-call.html.

18. Joseph M. Stowell, *The Weight of Your Words: Measuring the Impact of What You Say* (Chicago: Moody, 1998), defines slander as "the intentional sharing of damaging information" (40). But this definition lacks the needed clarity. For something to be slander, it can't merely be damaging; it also has to be *untrue*.

19. For more, see Kate Shellnutt, "Why Defining Gossip Matters in the Church's Response to Abuse," *Christianity Today*, April 20, 2021, https://www.christianitytoday.com/ct/2021/may-june/gossip-bible -definition-response-abuse-criticism.html.

20. Alan Stucky, "Stop Living in Fear of a False Report," *Dove's Nest*, June 23, 2016, https://dovesnest.net/Stop-Living-in-Fear-of-a-False -Report. Stuckey refers to the report of the National Sexual Violence

Resource Center (NSVRC): https://www.nsvrc.org/publications/false-reporting-overview.

21. Ed Pilkington, "Donna Rotunno: The Legal Rottweiler Leading Harvey Weinstein's Defense," *Guardian*, February 9, 2020, https://www.theguardian.com/film/2020/feb/09/donna-rotunno-lawyer-leading-harvey-weinsteins-defense.

22. Pilkington, "Donna Rotunno."

23. Leslie Vernick in Brad Hambrick, ed., *Becoming a Church That Cares Well for the Abused* (Nashville: Broadman and Holman, 2019), 116.

24. Leslie Vernick in Hambrick, *Becoming a Church*, 116.

25. Leslie Vernick in Hambrick, *Becoming a Church*, 116.

26. Hambrick, *Becoming a Church*, 107-120.

27. Bradley Campbell and Jason Manning, *The Rise of Victimhood Culture: Microaggressions, Safe Spaces, and the New Culture Wars* (New York: Palgrave Macmillan, 2018).

28. Wade Mullen, *Something's Not Right: Decoding the Hidden Tactics of Abuse and Freeing Yourself from Its Power* (Carol Stream, IL: Tyndale, 2020), 141–142.

29. J. R. R. Tolkien, *The Two Towers* (New York: HarperCollins, 1999), 223.

30. Mullen, *Something's Not Right*, 92.

CHAPTER 6: SUFFERING IN SILENCE

1. From the movie *Return of the King* (New Line Cinema, 2003). For the version in the book, see J. R. R. Tolkien, *The Return of the King* (New York: Ballantine, 1965), 331.

2. Tolkien, *Return of the King*, 382.

3. Lisa Oakley and Justin Humphreys, *Escaping the Maze of Spiritual Abuse: Creating Healthy Christian Cultures* (London: SPCK, 2019), 72–74.

4. F. Remy Diederich, *Broken Trust: A Practical Guide to Identify and Recover from Toxic Faith, Toxic Church, and Spiritual Abuse* (Columbia, SC: LifeChange, 2017), 101–104.

5. Diederich, *Broken Trust*, 116.

6. Diederich, *Broken Trust*, 92–93. For a helpful analysis of PTSD from a Christian perspective, see Greg E. Gifford, *Helping Your*

Family through PTSD (Eugene, OR: Wipf and Stock, 2017);
Paul Randolph, "Post Traumatic Distress," *Journal of Biblical
Counseling* 25, no. 3 (Summer 2007): 8–15; and Curtis Solomon,
"Counseling Post-Traumatic Stress Disorder: Plotting the Course,"
Association of Certified Biblical Counselors, October 24, 2019,
https://biblicalcounseling.com/resource-library/essays/counseling-post
-traumatic-stress-disorder-plotting-the-course/.

7. The National Institute of Mental Health, as cited in Gifford, *Helping
Your Family through PTSD*, 7.

8. Carly Parnitzke Smith and Jennifer Freyd, "Institutional Betrayal,"
American Psychologist 69, no. 6 (September 2014): 575–87, https://doi
.org/10.1037/a0037564.

9. Smith and Freyd, "Institutional Betrayal," 577.

10. Bessel van der Kolk, *The Body Keeps the Score: Brain, Mind, and Body
in the Healing of Trauma* (New York: Viking, 2014).

11. Van der Kolk, *Body Keeps the Score*, 46.

12. Van der Kolk, *Body Keeps the Score*, 46.

13. Van der Kolk, *Body Keeps the Score*, 54.

14. Van der Kolk, *Body Keeps the Score*, 55.

15. Van der Kolk, *Body Keeps the Score*, 54.

16. Van der Kolk, *Body Keeps the Score*, 89–90.

17. Chuck DeGroat, *When Narcissism Comes to Church: Healing Your
Community from Emotional and Spiritual Abuse* (Downers Grove, IL:
InterVarsity Press, 2020), 138; Diederich, *Broken Trust*, 92–93.

18. Brendan Kiley, "Why the Mars Hill Faithful Have Started to
Question Mark," *Stranger*, July 30, 2014, https://www.thestranger
.com/seattle/why-the-mars-hill-faithful-have-started-to-question
-mark/Content?oid=20257920.

19. Kate Shellnutt, "Acts 29 CEO Removed Amid 'Accusations
of Abusive Leadership,'" *Christianity Today*, February 7, 2020,
https://www.christianitytoday.com/news/2020/february/acts-29-ceo
-steve-timmis-removed-spiritual-abuse-tch.html.

20. Oakley and Humphreys, *Escaping the Maze*, 83.

21. Kenneth J. Garrett, *In the House of Friends: Understanding and
Healing from Spiritual Abuse in Christian Churches* (Eugene, OR:
Wipf and Stock, 2020), 63.

22. Wade Mullen, *Something's Not Right: Decoding the Hidden Tactics of Abuse and Freeing Yourself from Its Power* (Carol Stream, IL: Tyndale, 2020), 181.

23. Mullen, *Something's Not Right*, 181.

24. Diederich, *Broken Trust*, 111.

25. Diederich, *Broken Trust*, 58.

26. Oakley and Humphreys, *Escaping the Maze*, 67–68.

27. Oakley and Humphreys, *Escaping the Maze*, 77–78.

28. Diederich, *Broken Trust*, 89.

29. David Johnson and Jeff VanVonderen, *The Subtle Power of Spiritual Abuse: Recognizing and Escaping Spiritual Manipulation and False Spiritual Authority within the Church* (Minneapolis: Bethany House, 1991), 42–43.

30. Oakley and Humphreys, *Escaping the Maze*, 75.

31. *An Independent Learning Review: The Crowded House*, October 26, 2020, Thirtyone:eight, 12, https://thirtyoneeight.org/media/2678/the -crowded-house-learning-review-full-report.pdf.

CHAPTER 7: THEY SHALL NOT HURT OR DESTROY

1. John Dillenberger, ed., *Martin Luther: Selections from His Writings* (New York: Doubleday, 1962), 429.

2. "On the Protection of Towns from Fire," *Pennsylvania Gazette*, February 4, 1734/35, in Leonard W. Labaree, ed., *The Papers of Benjamin Franklin, Volume 2: January 1, 1735, through December 31, 1744* (New Haven: Yale University Press, 1961), 12–15.

3. I realize that for many Presbyterian denominations, the pastor is the *ex officio* moderator of the session. But this doesn't mean he has to set the agenda; that can be delegated to others.

4. Rather than members rolling off the elder board, an alternative would be to shuffle the makeup of various elder committees.

5. See the report at https://www.pcahistory.org/pca/studies/2017_WIM .pdf.

6. Jamie Dunlop, "Should Elders Insist on Unanimity?," 9Marks, October 28, 2018, https://www.9marks.org/article/should-elders-insist -on-unanimity/.

7. Lisa Oakley and Kathryn Kinmond, *Breaking the Silence on Spiritual Abuse* (New York: Palgrave Macmillan, 2013), 28–30.

8. David Johnson and Jeff VanVonderen, *The Subtle Power of Spiritual Abuse: Recognizing and Escaping Spiritual Manipulation and False Spiritual Authority within the Church* (Minneapolis: Bethany House, 1991), 67.

9. Westminster Confession of Faith, 31.3, http://files1.wts.edu/uploads /pdf/about/WCF_30.pdf.

10. Julie Roys, "Indiana Presbytery Will Put Pastor Accused of Sexual Abuse on Trial," *Roys Report*, May 17, 2021, https://julieroys.com /indiana-presbytery-sexual-abuse-trial/.

11. Jackson Elliott, "Former Members of Indiana Church Accuse Pastor of Sexual Abuse and Presbytery of Covering It Up," *Roys Report*, May 12, 2021, https://julieroys.com/pastor-accused-of-sexual -abuse-cover-up/.

12. Elliott, "Former Members of Indiana Church Accuse Pastor of Sexual Abuse."

13. Elliott, "Former Members of Indiana Church Accuse Pastor of Sexual Abuse."

14. Roys, "Indiana Presbytery Will Put Pastor Accused of Sexual Abuse on Trial."

15. Boz Tchividjian, "Are Abuse Survivors Best Served When Institutions Investigate Themselves?," *Religion News Service*, October 16, 2015, https://religionnews.com/2015/10/16/are-abuse-survivors-best -served-when-institutions-investigate-themselves/.

EPILOGUE

1. David Johnson and Jeff VanVonderen, *The Subtle Power of Spiritual Abuse: Recognizing and Escaping Spiritual Manipulation and False Spiritual Authority within the Church* (Minneapolis: Bethany House, 1991), 75–76.

2. Thomas Watson, *The Godly Man's Picture Drawn with a Scripture Pencil, or, Some Characteristic Marks of a Man Who Is Going to Heaven* (Carlisle, PA: Banner of Truth, 1992), 79.

3. Matt Smethurst, "Hard to Offend, Easy to Please: How Love Hopes All Things," Desiring God, June 30, 2021, https://www.desiringgod .org/articles/hard-to-offend-easy-to-please.

4. C. S. Lewis, *The Voyage of the Dawn Treader* (New York: Harper Collins, 1952), 92.

5. Lewis, *Voyage of the Dawn Treader*, 92.

6. As cited in *Star Wars: Revenge of the Sith* (2005).

7. Mike Cosper, "You Read the Bible, Ringo?," July 7, 2021, in *The Rise and Fall of Mars Hill*, produced by *Christianity Today*, podcast, quote at 40:00, https://www.christianitytoday.com/ct/podcasts/rise-and-fall -of-mars-hill/rise-fall-mars-hill-podcast-bible-ringo.html.